ICDS 2023

The Seventeenth International Conference on Digital Society

April 24th – 28th, 2023

Venice, Italy

ICDS 2023 Editors

Olga Levina, Technische Hochschule Brandenburg, Germany
Lasse Berntzen, University of South-Eastern Norway, Norway

Printed from e-media with permission by:

Curran Associates, Inc.
57 Morehouse Lane
Red Hook, NY 12571

Some format issues inherent in the e-media version may also appear in this print version.

Printed with permission by Curran Associates, Inc. (2024)

International Academy, Research, and Industry Association (IARIA)
412 Derby Way
Wilmington, DE 19810

Phone: (408) 893-6407
Fax: (408) 527-6351

petre@iaria.org

Additional copies of this publication are available from:

Curran Associates, Inc.
57 Morehouse Lane
Red Hook, NY 12571 USA
Phone: 845-758-0400
Fax: 845-758-2633
Email: curran@proceedings.com
Web: www.proceedings.com

Table of Contents

ICDS 2023

Forward

The Seventeenth International Conference on Digital Society (ICDS 2023) was held in Venice, Italy, April 24 - 28, 2023.

Nowadays, most of the economic activities and business models are driven by the unprecedented evolution of theories and technologies. The impregnation of these achievements into our society is present everywhere, and it is only question of user education and business models optimization towards a digital society.

Progress in cognitive science, knowledge acquisition, representation, and processing helped to deal with imprecise, uncertain or incomplete information. Management of geographical and temporal information becomes a challenge, in terms of volume, speed, semantic, decision, and delivery.

Information technologies allow optimization in searching an interpreting data, yet special constraints imposed by the digital society require on-demand, ethics, and legal aspects, as well as user privacy and safety.

The event was very competitive in its selection process and very well perceived by the international scientific and industrial communities. As such, it is attracting excellent contributions and active participation from all over the world. We were very pleased to receive a large amount of top quality contributions.

The accepted papers covered a large spectrum of topics related to advanced networking, applications, social networking, security and protection, and systems technologies in a digital society. We believe that the ICDS 2023 contributions offered a panel of solutions to key problems in all areas of digital needs of today's society.

We take here the opportunity to warmly thank all the members of the ICDS 2023 technical program committee as well as the numerous reviewers. The creation of such a broad and high quality conference program would not have been possible without their involvement. We also kindly thank all the authors that dedicated much of their time and efforts to contribute to the ICDS 2023. We truly believe that thanks to all these efforts, the final conference program consists of top quality contributions.

This event could also not have been a reality without the support of many individuals, organizations and sponsors. In addition, we also gratefully thank the members of the ICDS 2023 organizing committee for their help in handling the logistics and for their work that is making this professional meeting a success.

We hope the ICDS 2023 was a successful international forum for the exchange of ideas and results between academia and industry and to promote further progress on the topics of digital society. We also hope that Venice provided a pleasant environment during the conference and everyone saved some time for exploring this beautiful city

ICDS 2023 Chairs

ICDS Steering Committee
Lasse Berntzen, University of South-Eastern Norway, Norway
Claus-Peter Rückemann, Westfälische Wilhelms-Universität Münster (WWU) / DIMF / Leibniz Universität

Hannover, Germany
Theo Lynn, Irish Institute of Digital Business, Dublin City University, Ireland
Olga Levina, Technische Hochschule Brandenburg, Germany

ICDS 2023 Publicity Chair

Laura Garcia, Universitat Politècnica de València (UPV), Spain
Javier Rocher Morant, Universitat Politecnica de Valencia, Spain

ICDS 2023

COMMITTEE

ICDS Steering Committee

Lasse Berntzen, University of South-Eastern Norway, Norway
Claus-Peter Rückemann, Westfälische Wilhelms-Universität Münster (WWU) / DIMF / Leibniz Universität Hannover, Germany
Theo Lynn, Irish Institute of Digital Business, Dublin City University, Ireland
Olga Levina, Technische Hochschule Brandenburg, Germany

ICDS 2023 Publicity Chairs

Javier Rocher Morant, Universitat Politecnica de Valencia, Spain
Laura Garcia, Universitat Politecnica de Valencia, Spain

ICDS 2023 Technical Program Committee

Chiniah Aatish, University of Mauritius, Mauritius
Mohamad Ibrahim Al Ladan, Rafik Hariri University, Lebanon
Laura Alcaide Muñoz, University of Granada, Spain
Mark Alfano, Macquarie University, Australia
Ludivine Allienne, Université Picardie Jules Verne - laboratoire CURAPP-ESS, France
Kambiz Badie, ICT Research Institute, Iran
Alessandra Bagnato, Softeam, France
Sanmitra Banerjee, NVIDIA, Santa Clara, USA
Ilija Basicevic, University of Novi Sad, Serbia
Najib Belkhayat, Cadi Ayyad University of Marrakech, Morocco
Lasse Berntzen, University of South-Eastern Norway, Norway
Aljosa Jerman Blazic, SETCCE Ltd. / IT association at Chamber of commerce, Slovenia
Mahmoud Brahimi, University of Msila, Algeria
Justin F. Brunelle, The MITRE Corporation, USA
Maria Chiara Caschera, CNR-IRPPS, Italy
Sunil Choenni, Dutch Ministry of Justice and Security / Rotterdam University of Applied Sciences, Netherlands
Yul Chu, University of Texas Rio Grande Valley (UTRGV), USA
Andrei V. Chugunov, ITMO University, St.Petersburg, Russia
Soon Ae Chun, City University of New York, USA
María E. Cortés-Cediel, Universidad Complutense de Madrid, Spain
Vladimir Costas-Jauregui, Universidad Mayor de San Simón, Bolivia
Arthur Csetenyi, Budapest Corvinus University, Hungary
Ibibia K. Dabipi, University of Maryland Eastern Shore, USA
Fisnik Dalipi, Linnaeus University, Sweden
Monica De Martino, CNR-IMATI (National research Council, Institute of applied Mathematics and Information technology), Italy
Alexander Dekhtyar, California Polytechnic State University, USA
Joakim Dillner, Karolinska University Laboratory | Karolinska University Hospital - Center for Cervical Cancer Prevention, Sweden
Ilie Cristian Dorobat, "Politehnica" University of Bucharest, Romania

Nancy Routzouni, University of Aegean, Greece
Claus-Peter Rückemann, Westfälische Wilhelms-Universität Münster (WWU) / DIMF / Leibniz Universität Hannover, Germany, Germany
Peter Y. A. Ryan, University of Luxembourg, Luxembourg
Niharika Sachdeva, IIIT-Delhi | Info Edge, India
Imad Saleh, University Paris 8, France
Iván Santos-González, University of La Laguna, Tenerife, Spain
Demetrios Sarantis, United Nations University, Japan
Kurt M. Saunders, California State University, Northridge, USA
Deniss Ščeulovs, Riga Technical University, Latvia
Andreas Schmietendorf, Berlin School of Economics and Law - University of Magdeburg, Germany
Thorsten Schöler, Augsburg University of Applied Sciences, Germany
M. Omair Shafiq, Carleton University, Canada
Navid Shaghaghi, Santa Clara University, USA
Andreiwid Sheffer Correa, Federal Institute of Education, Science and Technology of Sao Paulo, Brazil
Ecem Buse Sevinç Çubuk, Aydın Adnan Menderes University, Turkey
Åsa Smedberg, Stockholm University, Sweden
Evgeny Styrin, National Research University Higher School of Economics, Russia
Dennis S. Tachiki, Hosei University, Tokyo, Japan
Chrisa Tsinaraki, EU JRC, Italy
Taketoshi Ushiama, Kyushu University, Japan
Giacomo Valente, University of L'Aquila, Italy
Esteban Vázquez Cano, Universidad Nacional de Educación a Distancia (UNED), Spain
Genanew B.Worku, University of Dubai, UAE
Yuling Yan, Santa Clara University, USA
Yingjie Yang, Institute of Artificial Intelligence - De Montfort University, UK
Michele Zanella, Politecnico di Milano, Italy
Sergio Zepeda, Universidad Autónoma Metropolitana, Mexico
Qiang Zhu, University of Michigan - Dearborn, USA
Ewa Ziemba, University of Economics in Katowice, Poland

Taking the Matter in their own Hands – Can Business Unit Developers Fullfill their Digital Demands with Low-Code Development Platforms?

Katharina Frosch
Department of Economics
Brandenburg University of Applied Sciences
Brandenburg an der Havel, Germany
katharina.frosch@th-brandenburg.de

Olga Levina
Department of Economics
Brandenburg University of Applied Sciences
Brandenburg an der Havel, Germany
olga.levina@th-brandenburg.de

***Abstract*— Low Code Development Platforms (LCDP) often promise an easy and fast way to include data processing and support into the otherwise non-digital process. Nevertheless, it often remains unclear, besides anecdotal evidence, how business users are getting on with transformation of business requirements into the software. This research explores the potential low code development has for business users to address their needs for process support via software tools. The experiment was chosen as the research method to assess the feasibility of software development with LCDP by novices. The results point towards a dedicated LCDP implementation approach if the technology is to be implemented in the business context. Hence, the research provides suggestions on how Business Unit Developers (BUD) can be supported to efficiently deliver productive results and how to assess LCDP-based development process and points towards potential challenges of LCDP implementation.**

Keywords- low code development platforms; software development proces; digital novices; socially-aware software; performance indicators

I. INTRODUCTION

Routine data processing within a process can take up time, which might be required in a more expert context. Nevertheless, integration of a specific software or data layer might not be enough to start a development process due, among others, to the lack of resources in the developer teams.

Low Code Development Platforms (LCDP) promise an easy and fast possibility to include data processing and data exchange support in the otherwise non-digital process [1]. The terms "citizen developer" [2] or "business unit developer" [3] are often used in the LCDP context to underline the potential of the software tools to involve programming novices in the development of the solution for their needs [4].

LCDP allow platform users to develop applications based on a Graphical User Interface (GUI) without creating code and thus to develop programming skills [4]. Each GUI object is programmed in a hard code that can be adapted to some degree of personalization.

This research follows up on this promise with the goal of exploring the potential low code development has for business users to answer their need for support via software tools. The research questions were as follows: Are LCDP feasible for programming novices? And: What aspects need to be considered if an LCDP is provided for the user? Hence, this research provides suggestions on how Business Unit Developers (BUD) can be supported to efficiently provide productive results. This research was not previously published and is the first to be presented here.

The paper is structured as follows: First, the current literature on LCDP and its use in a business context is reviewed, and the research questions are derived in Section 2. Research methods description in Section 3 and results descriptions in Section 4 lead to recommendations on how to implement LCDP in productive environment. Section 5 provides summary and outlook on future research as a conclusion.

II. RELATED WORK

The use of the LCDP in different business domains has been increasingly the focus of research in the last years. Sanchis et al. [5] showed that rapidity and the cost reduction through intuitive development and management can be attributed to the LCDP in manufacturing context. Nowak et al. [6] show case the usage of LCDP in the context of the internal logistics processes in a company from the E-Commerce industry. This case study is meant to display the use of LCDP in the context of process improvement as is allows for direct eliminations of found limitations in processes. The authors argue that the implementation of the IT support using LCDP was effective, #, an enhancement in terms of time and costs needed for its realization.

Bies et al. [7] conduct a mixed-method study to identify challenges and promising perspectives for digital innovations in Small and Middle Enterprises (SME). The authors found the LCDP application areas are mostly of the supportive nature such as creation of application for resource management or creation of customized digital forms. Nevertheless, the majority of the surveyed SMEs stated LCDP to be of high to very high relevance. Factors that diminish the relevance for low-code in SME are according to the authors: limited human resources, as personnel is still necessary to develop and maintain the application, knowledge transfer between the platforms as well as training in dealing with IT structures and detailed knowledge of the platforms.

Lethbridge [8] also explores the development process of the software product as well as the aspects of implementation and maintenance of the LCDP software within the existing enterprise architecture. His findings suggest that LCDPs create "technical debts" that can be overcome by the development of the LCDP towards "scaling, understandability, documentarily, usability, vendor-independence and user experience for the developers". Hintsch et al. 2021 [9] also identify threats and opportunities in the LCDP development concerning the security and availability of the created applications. Nevertheless, the authors also uncover success factors for LCDP use in a business context by novices.

Kermanchi et al. [10] focus in their research on software development methods and the use of LCDP. In their experiment, they explored the episodic experience with different LCDP among software developers with varying levels of programming experience but no experience in the specific LCDP. The findings show that previous programming experience seems to have a significant impact on developers' performance, experience, and tool preferences, yet most developers continue to have doubts about the scalability and maintainability of applications created with LCDPs. Opinions on the effectiveness of the instruments vary among the participants.

Bernsteiner et al. [11], conduct expert interviews in their research to investigate what skills developers with little or no software development experience, i.e., novices, need to successfully develop software on LCDP platforms. Several of the interviewed experts mention that successfully developing an LCDP solution requires at least basic programming skills. This is in line with research findings stating that LCDPs still require some prerequisites in software development [12] or in database structures [13], which hampers the adoption of LCDP by non-programmers without any further training.

Krejci et al. [13] report in a case study how non-IT employees were involved in the process of digital innovation while making efficient use of their IT resources. These citizen developers, i.e., employees who are working outside of the Information Technology (IT) department and are not professional programmers, as users of LCDP are in the focus of the analysis by Lebens et al. [14]. The authors conducted a survey about the use of LCDP in organizations. The results show that companies both large and small are making use of low- and no-code platforms. Additionally, the majority of the surveyed organizations have employees outside of the IT department who are creating IT solutions.

Bock and Frank [15] provide a critical overview of the LCPD features, architecture, and opportunities, while pointing out research directions for information systems research in this domain. They state that although both professional developers and citizen developers use LCDP, there is a lack of research on how to make LCDPs fit cognitive capabilities and personal working styles of these two groups [p. 739]. This is in line with other studies pointing out that successfully developing software on LCDP requires at least basic programming skills.

The use of development templates in the context of software creation is analyzed by Boot et al. [16]. The authors compare instructional software products made by developers with low production experience and high production experience, working with a template-based authoring tool. The analysis showed that the technical and authoring quality was equal for both groups, indicating that templates enable domain specialists to participate successfully in the production process. Research in agile software development shows that SCRUM projects profit from having a coach on the team [17]. The same is visible in software engineering education [18].

BUD and job crafting, i.e., proactive strategies to improve work processes according to one's own needs and goals, are subjects of the analysis by Li et al. [3]. The authors found that using LCDP provides positive jobs crafting consequences such as meaningfulness, for the employees using these tools [3][19]. In what follows, we prefer to use the term BUD instead of citizen developers, stressing that they might make up for the lack of programming skills by their large expertise in the respective business domain. Nerveless, the research does not focus on the description of how much support was needed for BUD to finish their application.

Despite these first attempts to understand the "human side" of LCDPs, research is still scarce with respect to acceptance and successful adoption by domain experts outside corporate IT departments. To our knowledge, there are no empirical studies yet to gain a deeper understanding of how BUD fare when using LCDPs. With our study, we contribute to closing this gap and explore:

- Whether BUD can develop functional applications based on LCDPs to improve their business operations
- Whether the amount of time invested and developing behavior differ between BUD and IT experts when using an LCDP to develop applications

III. RESEARCH METHOD

To gain evidence for answering our research questions, we draw upon a field experiment where BUD and IT experts build apps in the business domain of Human Resource Management (HRM) based on an LCDP given a finite time frame of few weeks. The experiment was divided in three challenges with modified compositions of participants. The challenges are described below. For the experiment, BUD are Master students of business management with the specialization in HR (20 students). In the third challenge, BUD were included in teams with experts. The experts were Master students of Information Systems Research (ISR) (18 students). All of the ISR students had already taken at least one course in advanced software engineering within their master program at the time of the experiment, thus gaining the definition as "IT experts". None of the participants was familiar with or has heart of the LCDP selected for the experiment.

The LCDP used for the experiment was Joget [20], an open-source LCDP with the promise to easily build, run and maintain apps. A visual builder allows drag-and-drop for pages, forms, views, data lists, menus, and a process builder to automate workflows. It also offers user management and role-based authentication. We used the community edition that can be self-hosted at no license cost.

The experiment is divided into three self-contained challenges. Challenge #1 was run with a few BUD only, in order to have a pretest and check whether business students are, at all, able to use the LCDP to develop simple apps. The pretest was run between April 21 and June 6, 2021. To kick start app development, BUD were provided with links to tutorials as well as with a basic app template and a 30-min-video showing exemplarily how an app can be built starting from this template. In this context, they were also explicitly pointed to the open-source character of app development in this setting, and about the possibility to share and reuse app elements from other groups. In the pretest, BUD managed to develop apps, but pointed out that they would have enjoyed working in teams in order to solve problems collaboratively. Furthermore, support by one student who previously had graduated from a bachelor program in software engineering and acted as informal coach for his fellow students has been acknowledged as extremely helpful.

Based on the insights gained in the pretest, we recruited the informal coach from challenge #1 to act as a formally appointed coach in challenge #2 and decided to run development in teams. For Challenge #2: BUD teams (with three to four students) developed their apps within six weeks (April 21 – June 6, 2021, 42 days). The team members cooperated online, due to the restrictions because of the COVID-19 pandemic. Developers got the same kick start as in the pretest and were also pointed towards the template and the possibility to share and reuse apps. Furthermore, a coach with experience in software development was available to get help with questions on tool usage and minor development questions. In Challenge #3, expert teams (including four to seven students) developed their apps between May 20 and June 7, 2022 (19 days). During the development challenge, two teams joined forces within the development process, resulting in a seven members team working on the challenge. The first day of the development phase (May 20, 2022) was organized as a face-to-face daylong hackathon. The introductory video and tutorials were made available beforehand, but no template or coach were provided for the teams.

IV. Results

The experiment has shown that in all three challenges, BUD were able to create a software application using LCDP in a given amount of time without any additional training in software development. All 15 apps created during the challenges have been successfully developed and implemented. Successful means that they met the requirements depicted in the conceptual papers, and that apps worked when tested. The technology readiness of the resulting apps corresponds to level 3 (experimental proof of concept) according to the European Union Technology Readiness Levels [21].

To address the second research question, the logs were archived and anonymized to calculate time spent at the platform and number of actions taken to create an app. The development activities of challenge #2 and #3 were then compared using indicators for time spent on platform as well as number of actions taken (per developer and per app, respectively). Overall, our data comprises 320 logins by BUD and 206 logins by experts, resulting in 4895 and 4094 actions taken, respectively. Figure 1 shows that the distribution of time spent on the platform, logins and actions taken is right-skewed, with most developers investing not more than 10 hours in development. Moreover, in both the BUD and the expert group, we observe one outlier with more than 60 (BUD) and more than 30 (expert) hours, respectively. As comparing means given such a data structure may lead to misleading results, we use modal values to compare development activities between BUD and experts.

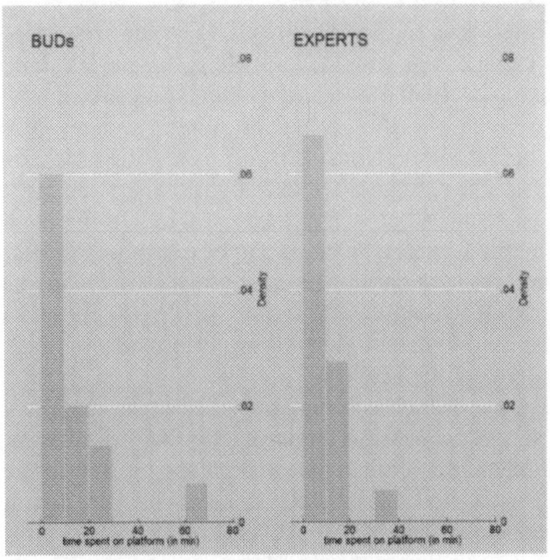

Figure 1. Time spent on platform

Table 1 shows that BUD tend to spend more time on the LCDP platform, but the total time investment per app is somewhat higher in the expert group. This result may be partly explained by the fact that on average, BUD teams were smaller than expert teams. BUD take fewer actions per app and per person as compared to experts. None of the indicators, however, shows statistically significant differences between the expert and the BUD groups when conducting a t-test on mean differences, also not when leaving out the extreme outlier in the BUD group (not displayed in Table 1).

TABLE I. Modal Values for Development Activity Indicators

Indicator	BUD	Experts
Time spent on platform (h), per developer	6.5	4.3
Time spent on platform (h), per app	23.7	30
Number of actions taken, per developer	152	165
Number of actions taken, per app	807	946

To conclude, we can state that BUD can create their own software applications in their business domain using an LCDP, and that time and effort invested in development are not significantly different from that of developers with programming knowledge.

V. Conclusion

The research question of this paper was whether LCDPs are a suitable tool for BUD to develop a digital solution that meets their requirements for information and data management within the business process without the involvement of the IT department. To answer this question, an experiment with three different challenges was conducted. All the solutions for the challenges led to an app that was ready to be implemented in the business context. Although, the quality of the created artifacts was not measured, and the size of the developer groups varied, the research offers valuable insights on the development process using LCDP by both non-IT and IT-trained users. Furthermore, some approaches were identified that might support BUD in the first steps during their engagement with the tool. Here, the use of templates and the availability of a coaching person is suggested.

In addition, this paper presented some indicators to measure LCDP performance within the software development process. The results can be used by managers and practitioners to support an effective and successful LCDP implementation. The applied research method can be expanded by HR and ISR researchers to support their conceptual artifacts in a low-code development context with data. Also, the suggested indicators can be used to assess the process performance of the software development with LCDP.

The experimental setting provided a near real life situation that allowed assessing the interaction with LCDP as well as resulted in interactional data that will be used to derive further insights on the LCDP-based business software development. Nevertheless, the group work made it more difficult to derive explicit indicators, so that future research will be based on individual software creation in collaborative stings. We will focus on the development of further interaction metrics for the assessment of the impact of LCDPs on the working styles of BUD and experts. Here, we will look at the engagement and interaction efficiency with the LCDP across the groups of experts and BUD. Another future research direction will focus on the job crafting effects of LCDP-based development for BUD and experts. Here, motivational and engagement aspects will be guiding the development of metrics to allow further comparative analysis.

REFERENCES

[1] S. Rafi, M. A. Akbar, M. Sánchez-Gordón, and R. Colomo-Palacios, "DevOps Practitioners' Perceptions of the Low-code Trend," *Int. Symp. Empir. Softw. Eng. Meas.*, pp. 301–306, Sep. 2022, doi: 10.1145/3544902.3546635.

[2] K. Rokis and M. Kirikova, "Challenges of Low-Code/No-Code Software Development: A Literature Review," in *Lecture Notes in Business Information Processing*, 2022, vol. 462 LNBIP, pp. 3–17, doi: 10.1007/978-3-031-16947-2_1.

[3] M. M. Li, C. Peters, M. Poser, K. Eilers, and E. Elshan, "ICT-enabled job crafting: How Business Unit Developers use Low-code Development Platforms to craft jobs," *ICIS 2022 Proc.*, Dec. 2022, Accessed: Feb. 03, 2023. [Online]. Available: https://aisel.aisnet.org/icis2022/is_futureofwork/is_futureofwork/16

[4] K. Talesra and N. G. S., "Low-Code Platform for Application Development," *Int. J. Appl. Eng. Res.*, vol. 16, no. 5, p. 346, May 2021, doi: 10.37622/IJAER/16.5.2021.346-351.

[5] R. Sanchis, Ó. García-Perales, F. Fraile, and R. Poler, "Low-code as enabler of digital transformation in manufacturing industry," *Appl. Sci.*, vol. 10, no. 1, p. 12, Dec. 2020, doi: 10.3390/app10010012.

[6] F. Nowak, J. Krzywy, and W. Statkiewicz, "Study on the Impact of the Use of No-code Application on Internal Logistics Processes in a Company from the E-Commerce Industry - Process Analysis," *Eur. Res. Stud. J.*, vol. XXV, no. Issue 2B, pp. 59–71, Aug. 2022, doi: 10.35808/ERSJ/2936.

[7] L. Bies, M. Weber, T. Greff, and D. Werth, "A Mixed-Methods Study of Low-Code Development Platforms: Drivers of Digital Innovation in SMEs," *Int. Conf. Electr. Comput. Commun. Mechatronics Eng. ICECCME 2022*, 2022, doi: 10.1109/ICECCME55909.2022.9987920.

[8] T. C. Lethbridge, "Low-Code Is Often High-Code, So We Must Design Low-Code Platforms to Enable Proper Software Engineering," *Lect. Notes Comput. Sci. (including Subser. Lect. Notes Artif. Intell. Lect. Notes Bioinformatics)*, vol. 13036 LNCS, pp. 202–212, 2021, doi: 10.1007/978-3-030-89159-6_14/COVER.

[9] J. Hintsch, D. Staegemann, M. Volk, and K. Turowski, "Low-code Development Platform Usage: Towards Bringing Citizen Development and Enterprise IT into Harmony," *ACIS 2021 Proc.*, Jan. 2021, Accessed: Feb. 06, 2023. [Online]. Available: https://aisel.aisnet.org/acis2021/11.

[10] A. Kermanchi, S. P. Fabian, F. Advisor, and A. Teronen, "Developer Experience in Low-Code Versus Traditional Development Platforms - A Comparative Experiment," Dec. 2022, Accessed: Feb. 03, 2023. [Online]. Available: https://aaltodoc.aalto.fi:443/handle/123456789/118413.

[11] F. Bernsteiner, R., Schlögl, S., Ploder, C., Dilger, T., and Florian Brecher, "Citizen vs. Professional developers: Differences and Similarities of Skills and Training Requirements for Low Code Development Platform," in *ICERI2022 Proceedings*, 2022, pp. 4257–4264.

[12] A. Sahay, A., Indamutsa, A., Di Ruscio, D., and Alfonso Pierantonio, "Supporting the understanding and comparison of low-code development platforms.," in *Euromicro Conference on Software Engineering and Advanced Applications (SEAA)*, 2020, pp. 171–178.

[13] D. Krejci, L. Küng, and S. Missonier, "A Case Study of Enterprise-wide Digital Innovation: Involving Non-IT Employees," *ECIS 2022 Res. Pap.*, Jun. 2022, Accessed: Jan. 23, 2023. [Online]. Available: https://aisel.aisnet.org/ecis2022_rp/55.

[14] M. Lebens, R. J. Finnegan, S. C. Sorsen, and J. Shah, "Rise of the Citizen Developer," *Muma Bus. Rev.*, vol. 5, pp. 101–111, 2021, doi: 10.28945/4885.

[15] A. C. Bock and U. Frank, "Low-Code Platform," *Bus. Inf. Syst. Eng.*, vol. 63, no. 6, pp. 733–740, Dec. 2021, doi: 10.1007/S12599-021-00726-8/FIGURES/1.

[16] E. W. Boot, J. J. G. Van Merriënboer, and A. L. Veerman, "Novice and experienced instructional software developers: Effects on materials created with instructional software templates," *Educ. Technol. Res. Dev.*, vol. 55, no. 6, pp. 647–666, 2007, doi: 10.1007/s11423-006-9002-9.

[17] C. Bunse, I. Grützner, C. Peper, S. Steinbach-Nordmann, and G. Vollmers, "Coaching professional software developers an experience report," *Softw. Eng. Educ. Conf. Proc.*, vol. 2006, pp. 123–130, 2006, doi: 10.1109/CSEET.2006.11.

[18] H. I. Akyüz and M. Kurt, "Effect of teacher's coaching in online discussion forums on students' perceived self-efficacy for the educational software development," *Procedia - Soc. Behav. Sci.*, vol. 9, pp. 633–637, Jan. 2010, doi: 10.1016/J.SBSPRO.2010.12.209.

[19] E. Elshan, E. Dickhaut, and P. Ebel, "An Investigation of Why Low Code Platforms Provide Answers and New Challenges," Accessed: Mar. 01, 2023. [Online]. Available: https://hdl.handle.net/10125/103380.

[20] Joget, "Open Source Platform to Easily Build, Run and Maintain Apps", Accessed: Mar 7, 2023. [Online]. Available: https://www.joget.org.

[21] European Commission, *Technology readiness levels (TRL)*, 2014, Accessed: Mar 7, 2023 [Online]. Available: https://ec.europa.eu/research/participants/data/ref/h2020/wp/2014_2015/annexes/h2020-wp1415-annex-g-trl_en.pdf

Mobile Instant Messaging and User Interface Design - Different Age Groups, Different Requirements?

A survey of Indonesian users

Olga Levina
Brandenburg University of Applied Sciences
Department of Management
Brandenburg an der Havel, Germany
levina@th-brandenburg.de

Abstract—**Instant Messaging (IM) is an increasingly popular form of communication in which two or more people exchange text-based multi-media messages in real time. However, as a result of aging, users have different needs and requirements towards the design of the communication application. This paper examines the preferences of users of different ages towards the User Interface (UI) design of Mobile Instant Massage (MIM) applications, i.e., instant message applications that can operate on smartphones. An online survey data about users' preferences towards the UI of this application type, limited to Indonesian users, was obtained. The results indicate that for some UI elements, both age groups showed the same preferences, while other requirements were significantly different. This paper aims to give a better understanding of the interface of the MIM application preferred by its users according to their age and thus inform application designers and product owners.**

Keywords: application requirements; usbality; user interface; age-based requirements; socially-aware information systems.

I. INTRODUCTION

With more than 3.5 billion smartphone users worldwide, their considerable proportion is constituted of so-called non-generic users such as children, older people and users with impairments. Hence, many applications and devices that are designed to cater to these users already exist. User Interface (UI) design is one of the most important aspects when developing a mobile device application, as the success of an application mainly relies on its usability and User eXperience (UX).

Instant Messaging (IM) can be seen as one of the first manifestations of digital communication technologies, which can reasonably be used as a substitute for real-life human interaction [1]. Being a text-based form of communication between two or more people exchanging text messages in real time, it can also provide asynchronous communication. Increasingly, it can be enriched with other forms of media such as pictures, videos, or audio files. For interpersonal exchanges, using instant messaging apps is associated with decreased feelings of loneliness for both young adults [2] and older users [3][4].

However, as a result of aging, adults have different needs and requirements for the design of communication applications compared with young people [5][6]. Current IM applications often design interfaces according to the needs of young people [7]. Based on these observations, this paper examines the user preferences of different age groups towards the User Interface (UI) design of Mobile Instant Massage (MIM) applications, i.e., instant message applications that can operate on smartphones.

An online survey was conducted. The user preferences analyzed in this paper will focus on two interfaces of the MIM application, namely, the message list and the messaging interface. The survey was distributed to Indonesian users. Sespiani and Ernungtyas [4] outlined a technological gap in Indonesia between age groups, as well as the difficulty in adapting to novel technologies for elderly Indonesian users. The results of the online survey indicate that for some UI elements, both age groups showed the same preferences, while other requirements were significantly different. This short paper aims to provide a better understanding of the interface of MIM applications preferred by its users, specifically Indonesian users. These insights are useful for designers, developers, and product managers of mobile messaging applications.

The paper is structured as follows: First, the current research on age-related UI preferences is described in section 2. The research method and results of the online survey are presented in sections 3 and 4 respectively. A discussion of the findings and further research directions are outlined in section 5.

II. STATE OF THE ART

IM is an internet service that allows users to communicate via text-based short massages directly in real time [8], while also allowing for asynchronous communication. In addition, IM allows users to share all types of messages, including video, sound, streaming content, web links, documents, and images [8][9]. The interface of IM is therefore focused on creating messages and displaying received massage, i.e., messaging and message list interface. A messaging interface is a UI where messages can be created and sent, as well as read and a voice over IP call can be associated.

The message list interface, mentioned as the main section of the IM application by Caro-Álvaro et al. [10], is where the feature chat management takes place. Furthermore, here received messages can be displayed, new messages can be created, individual or group messages can be pinned, among other functionalities. Given the focus on short, informal, unlimited, one-to many and many-to-many chat modes [9], as well as the charge-free [11] communication mode, IM applications are widely spread among smart phone users.

With the increase of user requirements and usage of mobile devices the number of UI guidelines also increases. Differences in UI requirements between different age groups have been abundantly discussed in research, e.g., in [12], [13]. Older users have been shown to exhibit difficulty understanding a series of tasks or actions in application menus designed for mobile applications [5]. Age-related aspects also lead to different UI interactions between the age groups [6]. Krayz et al. [7] showed UI mostly focuses specifically on the needs and recommendations of younger users to attract them. Hence, users frustrated with technology or who have difficulty learning technology will not be able to interact richly with the MIM application, thus often becoming dissatisfied with these applications [14].

Several age- related issues with UI design, as well as the potential solutions have been already discussed in research. Faisal et al. [15] show that the button design for mobile phones is unsuitable for the elderly, i.e. the buttons in the UI are too small. Similarly, many older users consider the positioning of the letters on the mobile keyboard as too dense, which exhibits a high error rate for text input [5]. Research by Kiat and Chen [9] shows that elderly users found the icons confusing and hard to identify. However, the choice of icons is not trivial as users from different demographics and cultures may interpret the same icon differently. The authors also state that that some older users have issues understanding the flow of existing MIM applications. Ahmad et al. [16] state that if it is confusing for older people to use the app, i.e., the application provides too many features, they become reluctant to use it.

Following these research insights, this paper explores the requirements for MIM messaging interface between different age groups using an online survey distributed among Indonesian users.

III. Research Method

In developing countries, such as Indonesia, older population is experiencing technological leaps [3]. As the average welfare increases, the availability of better infrastructure and increasingly affordable technology for people in Indonesia is also rising. Even though digital technology has become increasingly affordable, elder users in Indonesia have experienced a wide technological gap [4]. Due to a lack of skills and knowledge of technology, the motivation of older users to grapple with the understanding of IT is moderate. Thus, a further gap in technology understanding and user competence between older and younger generations is persistent [3].

Hence, the research question here is: What are the preferences of the younger users, those aged 20-30 years, and older users, those aged 50-60 years, toward the message list interface of an IM application? Specifically, to:

a. create a new message,
b. mark an individual or group message, and
c. see online-status information.

To answer this question, an online survey was created based on the results of usability research and recommendations described above. The survey included text-based questions, as well as A/B-test images to better understand the usability requirements. The online survey was designed using Google Forms and consists of four sections. The first section surveys for the demographics of the respondents. Also, some geographical data such as place of residence was gathered, as MIM preferences often depend on the region [11]. The second section collects the experience of the respondents on using the MIM applications.

The last two sections of the survey consist of questions that could summarize the respondent's preferences for the UI of MIM applications. Thus, they have three subsections that address each subitem of the research question. The first subsection collects the requirements for the preference for the button to create a new message (see Figure 1). Two types of floating action buttons were suggested (buttons A and B), as well as button C following the suggestion by Barros et al. [17], to add text on an icon button to increase the understanding of users towards the function of the feature.

Figure 1. Selection of "create new message" buttons

Then, the respondents are asked to choose an icon to pin or mark an individual or group message as a favorite. The first option is a pin icon, according to the function "pin a message," the second option is a star icon. The last option is the bookmark icon.

Finally, the requirements regarding the message list interface are surveyed. The focus is to find the respondents' preferences in viewing the online status of their contacts. Ogar et al. [14] stated that viewing the online status of the user's contacts is a concept of social presence.

First, the importance of the online status visibility is questioned. Then, the respondents are asked whether they would like to have the contact's online status available on the message list interface. This question collects the responses through a 5-point Likert scale, ranging from "strongly dislike" to "strongly like". Next, the participants are asked about how helpful it was to see people's online status on the message list interface (Figure 2).

Figure 2. Overview of potential message interfaces for MIM

The different possibilities of the indication of the online status are visible in Figure 2. The left and right screen show the status in the message overview, while the screen in the middle provides the status information in the dedicated chat.

IV. Results

A total of 150 Indonesian MIM users participate in the online survey. Among the respondents, 75 users are aged 20-30 years old (group A) and 75 users are in the age group of 50 and 60 years old (group B). From the results obtained, 66 respondents identified themselves as male, and 84 as female. The countries where the respondents live vary, although the majority (112 out of 150 respondents) live in Indonesia. Others live in Germany, Australia, United States of America, and Canada. Regarding the type of the operation system on their mobile device used by respondents, 72 respondents use Android and 78 use iOS- based devices.

A total of 149 survey participants stated that they use WhatsApp as their MIM. The second most used application by the respondents is Line, with 29 people, 25 respondents used Telegram, and 20 people used Facebook Messenger to communicate. When asked how self-explanatory the features in the MIM were, most of the features were rated as self-explanatory (see Figure 3).

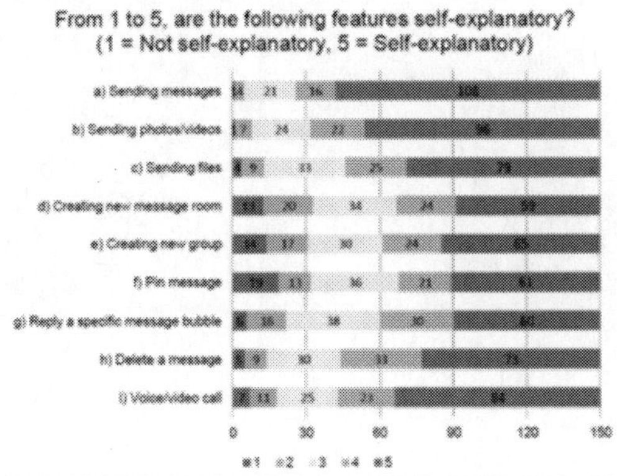

Figure 3. Understanding of the MIM features

Hence, the most self-explanatory feature is sending messages, while the feature that is the least self-explanatory is "pin messages".

When asked to rate the need for a user manual on a scale from 1 "not at all" to 5 "very much needed", the responses of different age groups varied significantly. With an average 2.44 for older users (group B) an average of 1.70 for young users (group A), group B was more likely to have an additional explanation of the application and its functions.

To assess UI preferences a 5 point Likert scale was used with 1= "very dissatisfied" to 5 = "very satisfied" with a specific feature or option. The position of the floating button on the top bar of the MIM application to create new messages was equally satisfactory for both age groups. Group A showed an average satisfaction of 3.96 and group B of 3.92. Significant differences between the button preferences for the function "create new message" (see Figure 1) were also visible: group B prefers button B, with an average of 2.01, while group A (younger users) are not clear for the preference between button A or B with an average of 1.75.

In addition, for the function of marking the message as favorite, group B preferred the start, while group A preferred a pin. Both age groups have similar preferences for the visibility of the online status of their contacts, with the average importance rated as 3.24 for younger users and 3.45 for older users.

Nevertheless, the importance of where the online status of contacts is displayed differs among age groups. The visibility of the online status in the message list is significantly more important for older users (group B) with an average importance of 3.52 than for younger users, with an average of 3.04.

Both age groups find it equally helpful to see online status in the message list interface, with an average of 3.55 (group A) and 3.63 (group B).

V. Conclusion

This research analyzed the UI requirements for MIM applications depending on the age of the users. An online survey was conducted, with 150 responses to answer the question about the preferences of the younger users and older users toward the message list interface of an IM application. The analysis of the results showed that for some UI elements, both age groups had the same preferences, while other features were met with different preferences.

Regarding the preferences for the button to create a new message in the message list interface, younger and older users preferred the button at the top bar over the floating action button. Each age group had different opinions on the type of button used for this feature. Button A was equally preferred by both age groups, while button B (chat bubble) and button C (text marker) were more preferred by younger and older users respectively. In terms of the function of marking a message as favorite, both age groups prefer to place the option to do that besides the swiped chat. However, each age group has a different icon choice that suits them better. Younger users like the pin icon better, whereas older users find the star icon more suitable. Finally, regarding seeing people's online status in the message list interface, more of the older users liked and found it helpful to have the online status in the message interface.

This analysis provided some insights into the usability factors that can help design user-friendly and efficient user interfaces for MIM in different age groups. These insights can be used by product owners and application developers to adopt their products to the aging population and minimize the inconveniences experienced by older users.

Acknowledgements: This research was based on data collected by Jennifer Surjanto.

REFERENCES

[1] C. A. Bardi and M. F. Brady, "Why shy people use instant messaging: Loneliness and other motives," *Comput. Human Behav.*, vol. 26, no. 6, pp. 1722–1726, Nov. 2010, doi: 10.1016/J.CHB.2010.06.021.

[2] E. Fumagalli, M. B. Dolmatzian, and L. J. Shrum, "Centennials, FOMO, and Loneliness: An Investigation of the Impact of Social Networking and Messaging/VoIP Apps Usage During the Initial Stage of the Coronavirus Pandemic," *Front. Psychol.*, vol. 12, p. 211, Feb. 2021, doi: 10.3389/FPSYG.2021.620739/BIBTEX.

[3] Restyandito, Febryandi, K. A. Nugraha, and D. Sebastian, "Mobile Social Media Interface Design for Elderly in Indonesia," 2020, pp. 79–85.

[4] K. A. Sespiani and N. F. Ernungtyas, "Connecting Elderly and Digital Devices: a Literature Review of User Interface Studies for Indonesian Elders," *J. Soc. Media*, vol. 6, no. 1, 2022.

[5] C. Dodd, R. Athauda, and M. T. P. Adam, "Designing user interfaces for the elderly: A systematic literature review," 2017, Accessed: Mar. 06, 2023. [Online]. Available: https://aisel.aisnet.org/acis2017/61/.

[6] K. Chirayus and A. Nanthaamornphong, "A Systematic Mapping Review: Mobile User Interface Design Guidelines for the Elderly with Cognitive Impairments," in *2019 23rd International Computer Science and Engineering Conference (ICSEC)*, Oct. 2019, pp. 35–42, doi: 10.1109/ICSEC47112.2019.8974698.

[7] K. Krayz Allah, N. A. Ismail, and M. Almgerbi, "Designing web search UI for the elderly community: a systematic literature review," *J. Ambient Intell. Humaniz. Comput.*, Jan. 2021, doi: 10.1007/s12652-020-02772-8.

[8] R. Bridgewater and M. Cole, *Instant Messaging Reference: A Practical Guide*. Elsevier Science, 2008.

[9] B. W. Kiat and W. Chen, "Mobile Instant Messaging for the Elderly," *Procedia Comput. Sci.*, vol. 67, pp. 28–37, 2015, doi: 10.1016/j.procs.2015.09.246.

[10] S. Caro-Álvaro, E. García-López, A. García-Cabot, L. De-Marcos, and A. Domínguez-Díaz, "Applying usability recommendations when developing mobile instant messaging applications," *IET Softw.*, vol. 16, no. 1, pp. 73–93, Feb. 2022, doi: 10.1049/sfw2.12039.

[11] H.-Y. Wang, "A Review of Instant Messaging and Mobile Messaging Applications," *Int. J. Econ. Financ. Manag. Sci.*, vol. 7, no. 1, p. 13, 2019, doi: 10.11648/j.ijefm.20190701.13.

[12] S. Sharma, "Age Based User Interface In Mobile Operating System," *Int. J. Comput. Sci. Eng. Appl.*, vol. 2, no. 2, pp. 177–184, May 2012, doi: 10.5121/ijcsea.2012.2215.

[13] J. J. Chang, N. S. Hildayah binti Zahari, and Y. H. Chew, "The Design of Social Media Mobile Application Interface for the Elderly," in *2018 IEEE Conference on Open Systems (ICOS)*, Nov. 2018, pp. 104–108, doi: 10.1109/ICOS.2018.8632701.

[14] S. O. Ogara, C. E. Koh, and V. R. Prybutok, "Investigating factors affecting social presence and user satisfaction with Mobile Instant Messaging," *Comput. Human Behav.*, vol. 36, pp. 453–459, Jul. 2014, doi: 10.1016/j.chb.2014.03.064.

[15] M. Faisal, N. Romli, and M. Faiz Mohamed Yusof, "Design for Elderly Friendly: Mobile Phone Application and Design that Suitable for Elderly," *Int. J. Comput. Appl.*, vol. 95, no. 3, pp. 28–31, Jun. 2014, doi: 10.5120/16576-6261.

[16] B. Ahmad, I. Richardson, and S. Beecham, "Usability Recommendations for Designers of Smartphone Applications for Older Adults: An Empirical Study," in *Software Usability*, IntechOpen, 2022.

[17] A. C. de Barros, R. Leitão, and J. Ribeiro, "Design and Evaluation of a Mobile User Interface for Older Adults: Navigation, Interaction and Visual Design Recommendations," *Procedia Comput. Sci.*, vol. 27, pp. 369–378, 2014, doi: 10.1016/j.procs.2014.02.041.

Decision-Support Systems and Decision Making: Managing Decisional Deskilling in Human-DSS Interactions in Organizations

A Quantitative Study

Nadine-Christine Wessel
Department of Business and Management
Technische Hochschule Brandenburg
Brandenburg an der Havel, Germany
e-mail: nadinechristine.wessel@th-brandenburg.de

Abstract—**The loss of individual decision-making skills and knowledge, also known as Decisional Deskilling, constitutes a significant threat to knowledge workers in the interactions with intelligent Decision-Support Systems (iDSS). The study used an online survey to test six hypotheses for examining the relationship between the extent use of intelligent decision-support systems and the impact on financial professionals' knowledge. The findings support the idea that extensive iDSS use decreases declarative and procedural knowledge. Therefore, balancing technology use with preserving employee skills and knowledge is vital. Proposed mitigation techniques include training and support programs, monitoring reliance on iDSS, and reevaluating system effectiveness.**

Keywords-decisional deskilling; artificial intelligence; decision-support systems; financial services; mitigation techniques.

I. INTRODUCTION

The increasing adoption of intelligent Decision-Support Systems (iDSS) in various industries, including healthcare and finance, has raised concerns regarding their impact on knowledge workers and their decision-making skills [1]-[3].

Decision-Support Systems (DSS) encompass any computerized system that assists with decision-making in organizations [4]. Emerging technologies, such as artificial intelligence have influenced the current DSS landscape [5], demanding a concept extension of the research field into iDSS. Artificial Intelligence (AI), which is also known as "machine intelligence", is a field in computer science that aims to develop systems capable of performing tasks that typically require human intelligence [6]. By using algorithms to learn from data, Machine Learning (ML) enables task automation [6]. According to [7] decision-making processes in organizations include 1) issue identification and problem finding, 2) decision question specification and problem formulation, 3) alternative generation and evaluation, 4) choice and 5) implementation. An iDSS that uses ML can perform any or all these phases. Despite the widespread use of DSS, there is limited research on the impact of iDSS on decision-making under these novel conditions [7][8].

iDSS implementation in organizations alters individual information processing and decision making [9] and can cause unintended deskilling [10]. This study defines this phenomenon as Decisional Deskilling (DD), which involves a decline in decision-making abilities and knowledge loss [1][11]. Literature suggests that DD is often caused by over-reliance on technology, also known as automation bias [1][12]. One possible explanation is that humans tend to delegate the responsibility of information seeking and processing to iDSSs, resulting in reduced individual effort [13]. This can also affect decision-makers' declarative knowledge and procedural knowledge [14]. Declarative Knowledge (DK) is "the storage of fact and events," whereas the memory of Procedural Knowledge (PK) "is more like a technique applied when necessary" [15]. For effective decision making, both types of knowledge, i.e., knowing the "What" and the "How" of the specific task are relevant [15].

[16] discovered that DD may only become apparent when iDSSs are discontinued, even though it can occur on a latent level. Prior research has therefore mainly focused on reliance and its short-term effects. [1] explored the impact of iDSS on DM and defined reliance based on factors, such as user's experience level, problem complexity, familiarity with the iDSS, and cognitive fit. In a case study of a German bank group with a fully automated iDSS [2] found that loss of critical thinking, knowledge, and expertise, as well as misuse of the system, were unintended employee-related short-term effects. [14] used a qualitative approach to investigate partially automated iDSS and identified three factors that reduce auditors' DK and PK, namely, the extent to which the tool takes over routine tasks, the auditors' reliance on the tool, and the time spent with iDSS.

Expanding on [14] this study explores the relation between the extent use of iDSS and financial professional's knowledge. Objectives were to 1) identify contributing factors, 2) assess the impact on professionals' knowledge, and 3) inform mitigation strategies. The paper is organized as follows: Section II outlines the empirical method, Section III presents survey results, Section IV discusses findings and implications, and Section V concludes.

II. METHOD

The study adopted a quantitative empirical approach and employed an online survey for data collection. Figure 1 shows the research framework based on [14].

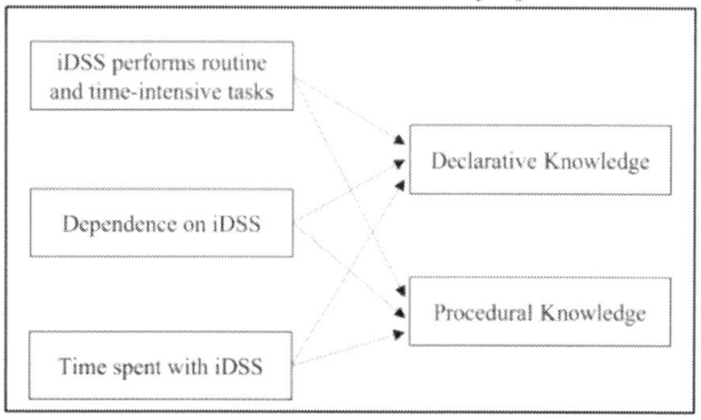

Figure 1. .Research Framework

A. *Sampling and Data Collection*

Sampling involved professionals from the financial services sector in Germany, encompassing investment banking, commercial banking, asset management, insurance, and other financial services. The additional criteria included experience in decision making, familiarity with DSS, and usage of partially or fully automated iDSS in their current role. These iDSS could be deployed to aid decision-making processes in risk management, fraud detection, portfolio management, credit scoring and underwriting, as well as financial forecasting and modeling. Data was collected through an anonymous online survey between 15th November to 15th December 2022, resulting in 39 completed questionnaires. The survey consisted of questions from the research framework, outlined in Table I, along with open-ended inquiries regarding access to training and support programs, and the participants' experiences with iDSS.

B. *Data Analysis*

To test the indicated relations of the three potential contributing factors and their impact on declarative and procedural knowledge, six initial hypotheses were built. The collected questionnaire data concerning the items for hypothesis testing were imported and computed using the software SPSS Statistics 28.0.1. In the first step, a null hypothesis and an alternative hypothesis were built for each of the hypotheses:

$$H_0: \rho = 0 \quad (1)$$

$$H_A: \rho \neq 0 \quad (2)$$

The Greek letter ρ indicates the population correlation, i.e., corresponding to the sample Pearson correlation coefficient r. The expression (1) of the null hypothesis H_0 means that Pearson coefficient equals zero, suggesting no association between the two tested variables. Based on the assumption that there is an association between the two variables, the alternative hypothesis H_A requires the coefficient to be different from zero as shown in (2). In the second step, the correlation coefficient r, two-tailed, was calculated and the strength of the correlation between both variables were determined according to Table II. In the next step, the statistical significance was determined by calculating the value of p. A relation is considered statistically significant if the calculated value of p is lower than alpha, with a predefined value of $\alpha < 0.05$. A qualitative content analysis and additional word frequency computations in R were used to examine the answers to the open questions.

TABLE I. QUESTIONNAIRE (EXCERPT)

Question	Item
Years of experience with IT tools for decision making?	Time spent with iDSS[a]
Which best describes the use of IT tools in your decision making?	iDSS performs routine &time-intensive tasks
How much do you feel that you rely upon IT-enabled support tools in carrying out your work?	Dependence on iDSS
Do you believe that your ability to recall details recorded in the IT tool (for example, customer data or financial data) is impacted as a result of your use of IT tool?	Declarative Knowledge
Do you believe that your ability to run your working tasks without the IT tools is impacted as a result of your use of the IT tools?	Procedural Knowledge

a. Multiple choice with single answer: 1) < 2 years, 2) 2 - 3 years, 3) 3 - 5 years, and 4) > 5 years
b. Multi select answers possible. Stages included: 1) Gathering information, 2) Identifying problems, 3) Developing options 4), Selecting the best course of actions, and 5) Implementing the decision.

TABLE II. THE SCALE OF PEARSON'S CORRELATION COEFFICIENT

Value of Coefficient *r*	Correlation
$0 \leq r \leq 0.1$	No Correlation
$0.1 \leq r \leq 0.29$	Low Correlation
$0.3 \leq r \leq 0.49$	Medium Correlation
$0.5 \leq r \leq 0.69$	High correlation
$0.7 \leq r \leq 1.0$	Very High Correlation

III. RESULTS

This study analyzed survey responses from 39 financial services professionals to determine the correlation and statistical significance among variables. The correlation results are summarized in Table III. Further insights were gathered from open questions on training and support programs, and participants' experiences with iDSS.

A. *Hypothesis Testing*

The study found significant correlations between "iDSS performs routine and time-intensive tasks" and "Declarative Knowledge", as well as "iDSS performs routine and time-intensive tasks" and "Procedural Knowledge", with medium effect sizes. These associations were statistically significant at the 0.05 level, indicating a probability of less than 5% that the null hypothesis, H_0, was correct. Thus, H_0 was rejected in favor of H_A, for both cases, providing support for hypotheses H_1 and H_2 as shown in Table IV.

Moreover, "Dependence on iDSS" showed a high correlation with both "Declarative Knowledge" and "Procedural Knowledge", with correlation coefficients of 0.63 and 0.66, respectively. These associations were statistically significant at the 0.05 level with a p-value of less than .001. As a result, H_0 was rejected in favor of H_A, providing support for hypotheses H_3 and H_4.

TABLE III. RESULTS OF CORRELATIONS

Contributing Factors	Declarative Knowledge N=39		Procedural Knowledge N=39	
	r	*p*	*r*	*p*
iDSS taking over decision making activities	**0.37**[a]	**.019**	**0.37**[a]	**.021**
Dependence on iDSS	**0.63**[a]	**< .001**	**0.66**[a]	**< .001**
Time spent with iDSS	-0.09	.588	-0.03	.853

a. Correlation is statistically significant at the 0.05 level (2-tailed)

TABLE IV. HYPOTHESES RESULTS

Hypothesis	Result
H_1 The greater the extent to which the iDSS performs routine and time intensive tasks, the less declarative knowledge possessed by the financial professional.	Supported $p = .019$
H_2 The greater the extent to which the iDSS performs routine and time-intensive tasks, the less procedural knowledge possessed by the financial professional.	Supported $p = .021$
H_3 The greater the financial professional's dependence on the intelligent system the less declarative knowledge possessed by the financial professional.	Supported $p = < .001$
H_4 The greater the financial professional's dependence on the intelligent system the less declarative knowledge possessed by the financial professional.	Supported $p = < .001$
H_5 The greater the time the financial professional has spent with the intelligent system, the less declarative knowledge by the financial professional.	Not supported $p = .588$
H_6 The greater the time the financial professional has spent with the intelligent system, the less procedural knowledge by the financial professional.	Not supported $p = .853$

However, the negative correlations that were observed between "Time spent with iDSS" and "Declarative Knowledge" as well as "Time spent with iDSS" and "Procedural Knowledge" were not statistically significant. Hence, H_0 could not be rejected for both cases, and thus, hypotheses H_5 and H_6 were not supported in the sample.

B. Training and Support Programs

The survey question on access to training and support programs for skill development in the working field found diverse responses. Some financial professionals have access to various programs, while others do not require any training due to fully automated software. Employers offer different types and modes of programs, such as internal academies with basic and advanced trainings, mentoring, and online courses, and some are setting up new programs due to the implementation of new software. Other participants reported that their employers offer soft skills, hard skills, and new technology training, as well as career development and coaching. Some also offer career consultation. Participants with access to training programs, stressed the importance of these programs in maintaining and improving skills. While some have access to technology-outdated programs, others do not use any offered by their employer.

C. Training and Support Programs

The finance professionals surveyed responded with a range of experiences and opinions on iDSS. Some found automation helpful in focusing on clients, while others felt pressure and risk of deskilling. The systems in place helped some organize their work, but others found the information superficial and not useful. Many said their organizations still had a traditional mindset despite technological changes, and they needed more training on the impact of new technology. Some found it challenging to understand the information provided by the software and explain their decisions. A few expressed concerns over the limited control they had over the software and its decisions. Some found automated systems convenient, but others found them difficult to navigate with overwhelming amounts of customer data. Difficulty in explaining decisions to other internal stakeholders due to the confusing solutions of systems and superficial answers to problems were also mentioned.

IV. DISCUSSION

The results showed significant associations between two of the three contributing factors and financial professionals' declarative and procedural knowledge, supporting four of the six hypotheses according to Table IV. The survey responses show a diverse range of experiences and opinions on iDSS, access to training and support programs for skill development.

A. Interpretation of the Findings

While some employers offer a variety of internal and external training and support programs, few participants have no access to training programs. Other participants feel they do not need them due to the ease of automated systems in place. Those with access emphasize their importance in maintaining and developing their skills. Some financial professionals appreciate technology's assistance, while others feel pressure to make quick decisions, struggling with the limitations and difficulty in navigating the systems in place effectively, and risking deskilling.

The results showed a significant association between financial professionals' dependence on the iDSS and a decrease in their DK and PK. In addition, there is a significant association between iDSS taking over routine and time-intensive tasks in decision making and a decrease in financial professionals' DK and PK. However, no significant association was found between time spent with the iDSS and DK and PK. Overall, the results suggest that a greater reliance on iDSS leads to a decrease in financial professionals' knowledge.

B. Theoretical and Practical Contributions

The theoretical contribution of this research lies in its examination of the relationship between the extent of use of iDSS and the knowledge possessed by financial professionals. By exploring this relationship, the study provided insights into potential contributing factors. The results indicate that the use of iDSS in organizations can notably influence the financial professionals` knowledge.

The findings of the study highlight the importance of striving for a balance between technology use and maintaining a capable workforce. Mitigation techniques to address DD include providing proper training resources and programs to support employee growth and development, as well as encouraging participation among employees. As AI becomes more prevalent in decision-making processes, monitoring employees' reliance on intelligent decision aids becomes crucial to identify areas where additional training and support is needed. By offering knowledge workers opportunities to participate in purely human decision making, organizations can further counteract the loss of specific task knowledge and skills. Finally, to ensure iDSS remains a supportive tool for decision making, the effectiveness of the system in place should be regularly reevaluated and information processes be adjusted accordingly.

C. Limitations

This study has several limitations that should be acknowledged. Firstly, the sample size of 39 finance professionals is relatively small, which may limit the generalizability of the results to other industries, organizations, or larger populations. Secondly, the findings of the study are based on the participants' own opinions and ratings, which may introduce some bias into the results. Additionally, these opinions and ratings are time-sensitive, which may impact the applicability of the results in the future. Lastly, this study only examined three contributing factors to decisional deskilling and did not consider other individual, technical, and organizational factors.

V. Conclusion and Future Work

By studying the relation between the extent use of iDSS and the knowledge possessed by financial professionals, the study found significant associations of the two contributing factors "iDSS takes over routine and time-intensive taks" and "Dependance on iDSS" with DK and PK. However, there was no significant association with the variable of "Time spent with iDSS". The results also revealed varied experiences and opinions on iDSS, as well as on participants' access to training and support programs. Some professionals appreciated technology's assistance, while others felt pressure to make quick decisions and struggled with the limitations of the IT tool in place.

The study highlights the potential drawbacks of over-relying on emerging technology for decision-making and emphasizes the need to mitigate potential negative impacts on workforce knowledge and skills. The results can be used to raise awareness of the significance of providing proper resources and programs to support employee growth and development, and to encourage organizations to invest in these resources. Mitigation strategies includes increasing participation in human decision-making activities, monitoring employees' reliance on iDSS, and reevaluating the effectiveness and efficiency of the system in place present further mitigation strategies to address DD.

Future research could benefit from a longitudinal study tracking the effects of DD over time and combining survey data with methods, such as interviews or case studies to gain a deeper understanding of the concept of DD.

Acknowledgment

The author likes to thank Olga Levina and the reviewers for their constructive feedback. Any opinions expressed in this article are those of the author.

References

[1] S. G. Sutton, V. Arnold, and M. Holt, "How Much Automation Is Too Much? Keeping the Human Relevant in Knowledge Work," J. Emerg. Technol. Account., vol. 15, no. 2, pp. 15–25, September 2018, doi: 10.2308/jeta-52311.

[2] A.-S. Mayer, F. Strich, and M. Fiedler, "Unintended Consequences of Introducing AI Systems for Decision Making," MIS Q. Exec., pp. 239–257, December 2020, doi: 10.17705/2msqe.00036.

[3] M. Schemmer, N. Kühl, and G. Satzger, "Intelligent Decision Assistance Versus Automated Decision-Making: Enhancing Knowledge Work Through Explainable Artificial Intelligence." arXiv, Sep. 28, 2021. [Online]. Available at: http://arxiv.org/abs/2109.13827. [retrieved: 6 April, 2023]

[4] R. Sharda, D. Delen, and E. Turban, Business intelligence and analytics: systems for decision support, 10th ed. Boston: Pearson, 2015.

[5] D. Arnott and S. Gao, "From Radical Movement to Organizational Mainstream: ABehavioral Economics Perspective on DSS History," in EURO Working Group on DSS, J. Papathanasiou, P. Zaraté, and J. Freire de Sousa, Eds., in Integrated Series in Information Systems. Cham: Springer International Publishing, 2021, pp. 239–257. doi: 10.1007/978-3-030-70377-6_13.

[6] V. B. Sowmya, B. Majumder, A. Gupta, and H. Surana, Practical natural language processing: a comprehensive guide to building real-world NLP systems, 1st ed. Sebastopol, CA: O'Reilly Media, 2020.

[7] D. J. Power, C. Heavin, and P. Keenan, "Decision systems redux," J. Decis. Syst., vol. 28, no. 1, pp. 1–18, January 2019, doi: 10.1080/12460125.2019.1631683

[8] D. Paradice, "Two Grand Challenges for DSS Evolution," in EURO Working Group on DSS, J. Papathanasiou, P. Zaraté, and J. Freire de Sousa, Eds., in Integrated Series in Information Systems. Cham: Springer International Publishing, 2021, pp. 33–49. doi: 10.1007/978-3-030-70377-6_3.

[9] V. U. Vincent, "Integrating intuition and artificial intelligence in organizational decision-making," Bus. Horiz., vol. 64, no. 4, pp. 425–438, July 2021, doi: 10.1016/j.bushor.2021.02.008.

[10] T. Hoff, "Deskilling and adaptation among primary care physicians using two work innovations," Health Care Management Review, vol. 36 no. 4, pp. 338–348, June 2011 doi:10.1097/HMR.0b013e31821826a1.

[11] R. Parasuraman, T. B. Sheridan, and C. D. Wickens, "A model for types and levels of human interaction with automation," IEEE Trans. Syst. Man Cybern. - Part Syst. Hum., vol. 30, no. 3, pp. 286–297, May 2000, doi: 10.1109/3468.844354.

[12] K. Goddard, A. Roudsari, and J. Wyatt, "Automation bias: A systematic review of frequency, effect mediators, and mitigators," J. Am. Med. Inform. Assoc. JAMIA, vol. 19, pp. 121–7, June 2011, doi: 10.1136/amiajnl-2011-000089.

[13] L. J. Skitka, K. L. Mosier, and M. Burdick, "Does automation bias decision-making?," Int. J. Hum.-Comput. Stud., vol. 51, no. 5, pp. 991–1006, November 1999, doi: 10.1006/ijhc.1999.0252.

[14] M. Axelsen, "Continued use of intelligent decision aids and auditor knowledge: Qualitative evidence" The 18th Americas Conference on Information Systems (ACMICS 2012), 5, 2012 pp. 3860-3869 [Online] Available at: https://aisel.aisnet.org/amcis2012/proceedings/AccountingInformationSystems/19. [retrieved: 6 April, 2023].

[15] T. ten Berge and R. van Hezewijk, "Procedural and Declarative Knowledge: An Evolutionary Perspective," Theory Psychol., vol. 9, no. 5, pp. 605–624, October 1999, doi: 10.1177/0959354399095002.

[16] T. Rinta-Kahila, E. Penttinen, A. Salovaara, and W. Soliman. (2018) "Consequences of Discontinuing Knowledge Work Automation - Surfacing of Deskilling Effects and Methods of Recovery," Proceedings of the 51st Hawaii International Conference on System Sciences, (HICSS 2018), March 2018, pp. 5244–5253, doi:10.24251/HICSS.2018.654.

Implementing the Cyber Security Act in Public Financial Institutions in Ghana

What are the Constraints and Enabling factors?

Emmanuel Awuni Kolog
Operations and MIS, University of Ghana
Accra, Ghana
Email: eakolog@ug.edu.gh

Tijani Mohammed
Operations and MIS, University of Ghana
Accra, Ghana
Email: mtijani003@st.ug.edu.gh

Abstract— **The Cyber Security Act of Ghana was enacted as a result of the National Cyber Security Policy and Strategy in Ghana. However, two years after its implementation, progress has been slow. This paper aimed to explore the constraints and enabling factors affecting the implementation of the Cyber Security Act in Ghana, based on the International Communication Union's pillars of cybersecurity. A mixed-method approach was used, with data collected from 168 respondents through a questionnaire and interviews. The survey data was analysed using Partial Least Square- Structural Equation Modeling (PLS-SEM), while the interview data was analysed using theory-based content analysis. The study found that financial institutions in Ghana have satisfactory policies and regulatory measures on cybersecurity, but lack the technical capacity to implement them effectively. The study also revealed satisfactory organizational and capacity development measures, but more awareness creation and organizational support are needed, including budget allocation and support from top management, to effectively implement cybersecurity policies in Ghana.**

Keywords- information security; cyber security act; public financial institutions; Ghana.

I. INTRODUCTION

Governments and organizations worldwide are increasingly utilizing Information and Communication Technologies (ICTs) to promote economic growth and national development [1]. However, the growing number of Internet users globally is hindering this progress. As of April 2022, there were over 5 billion active Internet users and approximately 1.92 billion websites, making cyber monitoring and control extremely difficult [2]. This development has also made cyberspace more susceptible to attacks and exploitation. Cybersecurity breaches can be catastrophic, resulting in loss of life, financial loss, and business collapse. Infamous cyberattacks, such as those on Sony Pictures, the USA pipeline shutdowns, and the NotPetya virus, for instance, were reported to have caused over US $10 billion in damages [3].

On December 29, 2020, Ghana's President assented to the 2020 Cyber Security Act 1038 [7]. The policy's aim is to provide a secure cyberspace to support the country's digitalization agenda and its transition to a knowledge-based economy. The Act draws on eight frameworks from Ghana's National Cybersecurity Policy and Strategy (NCSPS): legislative and regulatory frameworks, cybersecurity technology frameworks, culture of security and capacity building, research and development towards self-reliance, compliance and enforcement, child online protection, cybersecurity emergency readiness, and international cooperation frameworks [8].

The Act contains 100 sections and three schedules and assigns it to a Cybersecurity Authority (CSA) [8]. The CSA's objectives include regulating, managing, and promoting cybersecurity issues, as well as preventing and responding to cyber threats and incidents in Ghana. Sections 5 to 34 outline the CSA's structure, administrative provisions, financial provisions, and the establishment of a cybersecurity fund to support the authority's operations. Sections 41 to 48 provide for the establishment of national and sectoral computer emergency response teams (CERT) and cyber security incident reporting (CIRT). Licensing of cybersecurity service providers, accreditation of cyber professionals, and certification of cyber products are covered in Sections 49 to 58. The Act also promotes cybersecurity standards and their enforcement, public awareness and education as detailed in Sections 59 to 61.

As ICTs continue to fuel economic growth and national development, the number of active Internetusers worldwide has surpassed 5 billion, with over 1.92 billion websites as of April 2022 [2]. However, this increased digitalization has also made cyberspace vulnerable to cyber attacks, which can have severe consequences such as loss of life, financial loss, and business collapse. To address this, countries and organizations worldwide are now incorporating cybersecurity regulatory measures into their national and sectoral security strategies. In Ghana, the government is pursuing an ambitious digitalization agenda, which has led to increased cyber-related activities among government agencies, private sector institutions, and citizens. However, this has also led to an increase in cybercrime and cyber threats [5], such as ransomware, identity fraud, blackmail, online child exploitation, and social engineering.

This study aims to explore the implementation of Ghana's Cybersecurity Act 2020 (Act 1038) by public financial institutions and investigate the constraints and enabling factors needed to improve its implementation. The study is divided into six sections. Section I introduces the study and emphasizes the importance of the topic. Section II presents the study's framework and the development of its hypotheses. In Section III, the methodology is discussed, including data collection and analysis methods. Section IV presents the study's findings, while Section V interprets and discusses the results in depth. Finally, in Section VI, the paper concludes by summarizing the main points and drawing conclusions about the implementation of the Cybersecurity Act.

II. FRAMEWORK AND HYPOTHESIS DEVELOPMENT

In the section, we present the study's conceptual framework and **the** hypothesis development.

A. Framework

A comparative analysis of current international cybersecurity indexes by [10] [13] identified three key frameworks developed by cybersecurity experts and globally accepted for evaluating cybersecurity capacities: the Global Cybersecurity Index (GCI) by the ITU, the National Cybersecurity Index (NCSI) developed by the e-Governance Academy Foundation, and the Index of Cybersecurity (ICS) developed by the New York University Centre for Cybersecurity. Table I presents the GCI framework, which shows the various constructs.

TABLE I. MAPPING ITU MEASURES TO GHANA'S NCSPS

ITU Measures	Corresponding NCSPS Framework
Legal	▪ Policies and regulatory framework ▪ Compliance and enforcement measures ▪ Child online protection
Technical	▪ Cyber security technology framework ▪ Cyber security emergency
Organisational Capacity Development	▪ Effective governance ▪ Culture of security and capacity building ▪ Research and development towards self-reliance
Cooperation	▪ International cooperation

Although each framework seeks to measure cybersecurity capacities at the national and organizational level, their application and context vary because they have different systems of indicators and evaluation. The GCI is the most comprehensive and widely accepted framework, and it is used in this study.

B. Hypothesis Development

The legal measures, as presented in Table I, focus on the presence of legal and regulatory frameworks, which serve as the foundation of all cybersecurity policies. These measures provide clear guidance for cybersecurity governance and include indicators such as regulations for prosecuting cybercrime, protecting online identities and data, child online protection, privacy, system breaches, cybersecurity audits, implementation of standards, and identification and protection of Critical Information Infrastructure (CII) [10]. The implementation of these measures provides legal support in the form of policies and procedures that protect individuals and CII from exploitation and harm [11]. The question now is whether financial institutions are adapting to Ghana's 2020 Cyber Security Act 1038 or revising their existing policies to align with it. This leads to the first hypothesis of this study:

H1: *Financial institutions in Ghana have legal measures to implement cyber security Act*

The technical measures focus on the presence of structures and mechanisms to address cyber threats and incidents. This pillar acknowledges the significance of national and sectoral Computer Incident Response Teams (CIRT) and Computer Emergency Response Teams (CERTs) in promoting cyber resilience. Technical capacity also includes the existence of standards and baseline requirements for the deployment and use of technological resources. As technology is rapidly advancing, the technical capacity and technologies necessary to combat cybercrime and enhance national cybersecurity must also be continually improved to remain relevant. The 2020 Cyber Security Act 1038 contains provisions for establishing national and sectoral CERTs, CIRTs, and early warning systems, developing system standards, and capacity building [10]. Therefore, the study hypothesis is:

H2: *Financial institutions in Ghana have the technical capacity to implement cyber security Act*

The organizational measure examines the IT governance structures, including the establishment of cybersecurity objectives and strategic plans, as well as the formal definition of institutional roles and responsibilities to ensure accountability [10]. It assesses the existence of a central governing body and how it coordinates with various departments to implement and enforce these regulations. Key organizational indicators include the existence of a legitimate and enforcement authority; organizational cybersecurity strategies with an action plan; protection of Critical Information Infrastructure (CII); and a clear definition of roles and accountability for key stakeholders. Therefore, the third hypothesis for this study is:

H3: *Financial institutions in Ghana have organizational capacity to implement cyber security Act*

The *Capacity measure* involves activities required to increase human and institutional knowledge [10]. This measure supports the development of cybersecurity solutions to prevent and respond to threats and cyber risks. Under resource constraints environment, risk of cyber threats is higher because of absent or limited tools and technical knowledge [17]. Capacity building includes targeted awareness campaigns; a system for certification and accreditation of cyber security professionals and service providers; support for professional training packages in cybersecurity for key stakeholders; and the inclusion of cybersecurity in training programs. Other capacity-building measures also include research and development; the existence of a cybersecurity industry to support the development of cyber security products and services; and the growth of cyber start-ups. The study thus, hypothesize that:

H4: *Financial institutions in Ghana have developed a capacity building measures towards awareness of the Act.*

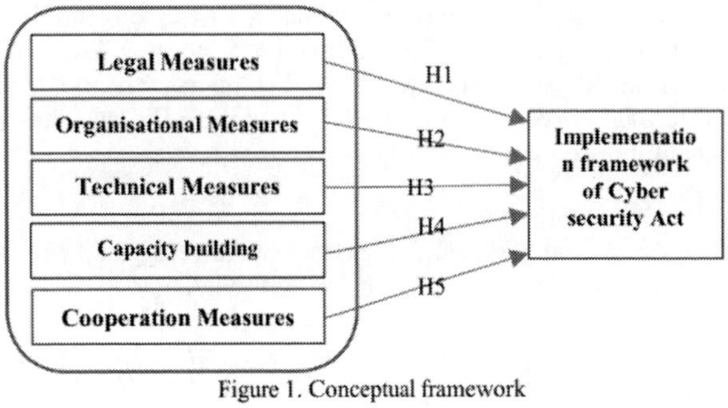

Figure 1. Conceptual framework

Cybercrimes are borderless and transnational; hence, promoting cybersecurity requires *collaboration and cooperation amongst* internal stakeholders and external agencies [17]. This requires a multi-stakeholder approach, including bilateral and multilateral agreements; participation of industry forums, international fora/associations; public-private partnerships; inter-agency partnerships; and alluring to best practices. This also assesses the number of partnerships, cooperative frameworks, and information-sharing networks established to build capacity and cyber resilience. Hence, we hypotheses that:

H5: *Financial institutions in Ghana are collaborating and cooperating to implement Act*

III. Methodology

The purpose of this section is to provide an overview of the approach and methodology used in the study

A. Research Approach and Data collection

A mixed research method was chosen for this study in line with its purpose. An empirical review was conducted to identify the constraints and enabling factors in the implementation of cyber security policies. The review revealed that a quantitative method combined with a qualitative approach would be the most appropriate way to gather data and insights from subject matter experts in the field of cybersecurity [13].

To achieve this, a survey questionnaire was developed along with structured interview questions for qualitative insights [14]. Efforts were made to ensure that the questionnaires relating to the hypothesis and conceptual framework could accurately ascertain discriminant validity and reliability [15]. The questionnaires used in this study were adapted from ITU's model questionnaires for cyber security evaluation (see Table II). Data was collected using online survey questionnaires and semi-structured interviews conducted simultaneously.

TABLE II. Mapping ITU Measures to Ghana's NCSPS

	Constructs	# of Items	Source
1	Legal measures	LM (7)	ITU-GCI, NCSSP
2	Technical measures	TM (7)	ITU-GCI, NCSSP
3	Organisational measure	OM (7)	ITU-GCI, NCSSP
4	Capacity measures	CD (5)	ITU-GCI, NCSSP
5	Cooperation measures	CM (4)	ITU-GCI, NCSSP

A purposive sampling technique was used, and survey links were sent to about 200 staff of financial institutions in Ghana. This provided a wide population reach to supplement the interviews conducted with 14 IT managers and chief information security officers (CISOs) from selected financial institutions.

B. Method of Data Analysis

A total of 154 valid responses were received from the survey, and data cleaning was performed. The data from the Likert scale were coded into numerical values for easy analysis. For close-ended responses, partial least squares structural equation modelling (PLS-SEM) was used for analysis. PLS-SEM is recommended for quantitative data analysis as it provides tools for estimating multiple and interrelated dependencies in a single analysis, which tends to provide a high level of predictive accuracy [16]. SmartPLS software was used as it is more feasible for measuring and developing comprehensive structural and predictive models.

IV. Results

The study's result is presented in this section.

A. Demorgraphic

Respondents spanned 12 banks and 4 rural banks in Ghana, with an average of 10 staff from each institution. 52 of the participants were females (34%) with the remaining being male (66%). For age distribution, there were distinct age groupings, which were Gen X, Gen Y, and Gen Z. Interestingly, the lowest level of education of the participants was bachelor's degree holders. Table III shows the summary statistic of the demographic data.

TABLE III. Participant Demography

Category	Variable	Frequency (N=154)	Percentage
Gender	Male	102	66
	Female	52	34
Age	18-23 years	6	4
	24-39 years	128	83
	40-55 years	20	13
Education	Bachelor	78	51
	Masters	76	49
Employment Level	Operational	90	58
	Middle mgt	52	34
	Top Mgt.	12	8

We assessed the respondent's knowledge of the Cyber Security Act in Ghana. From the results in Table III, 69% of participants were aware of the Act, with 31% not being aware. A question on cyber security attributes was asked by providing six options as follows: confidentiality, security, availability, protection, reliability, and policies. The respondents were tasked to select those that they know.

B. Cyber Act Implementation in Ghana

In using PLS-SEM to analyse the quantitative data, a 3-stage approach involving initial estimates of the measurement model and the structural model was developed, after which a final estimate for both the measurement and structural model was constructed.

1) Measurement Model Assessment

The latent variable with the indicators is reflective, hence, in its assessment, an analysis was conducted on the size and significance of the loadings, construct reliability, and convergent and discriminant validity [17]. The purpose of these assessment was to test for the relationship between indicators and constructs to ascertain their relevance. The initial step in measurement model assessment was to assess the indicator loadings of each construct. According to Hair *et al.* [12] loadings at 0.70 and above indicates that the construct explains more than 50% of the indicator's variance. As indicated in Table IV, some of the indicators were weak and deleted eventually.

An assessment of the reliability of the constructs was undertaken to identify the degree to which the indicators measuring the same constructs are related. This was done using Cronbach's alpha and composite reliability. However, for reflective PLS-SEM models, composite reliability is preferred to Cronbach's alpha because Cronbach's alpha can over or underestimate reliability due to its usage of the entire model for estimation [18]. Higher values indicate higher levels of reliability when interpreting construct reliability with a value at 0.70 and above preferred [16]. The composite reliabilities of the constructs in the research model are all above 0.70, indicating reliability among constructs to their indicators as shown in Table V.

After satisfying indicator and construct reliability, construct validity was performed to measure the extent to which the defined construct in the research model measures what it is intended to measure, such as legal measures truly measuring only legally related indicators. This assessment was done using convergent and discriminant validity.

TABLE IV. CONSTRUCT LOADINGS

	CD	CM	LM	OM	TM
CD2	0.912				
CD3	0.923				
CM1		0.870			
CM2		0.812			
CM4		0.902			
LM1			0.927		
LM2			0.906		
LM7			0.779		
OM1				0.969	
OM2				0.967	
TM1					0.903
TM2					0.912
TM3					0.919
TM5					0.903
TM7					0.932

Convergent validity examines if two interrelated constructs in the model are theoretically connected. This is also referred to as communality and it is measured with Average Variance Extracted (AVE). AVE value above 0.50 is always desired [20]. From Table V, all the constructs' AVE exceeds 0.50 which is above the desired threshold.

TABLE V. CONSTRUCT RELIABILITY AND VALIDITY

Constructs	Cronbach's Alpha	rho_A	Composite Reliability	AVE
Capacity	1.000	1.000	1.000	1.000
Cooperation	1.000	1.000	1.000	1.000
Implementation framework	1.000	1.000	1.000	1.000
Legal	0.843	0.871	0.905	0.762
Organisational	0.933	0.933	0.968	0.937
Technical	0.953	1.125	0.962	0.835

TABLE VI. HETEROTRAIT-MONOTRAIT RATION MATRIX=

	CD	CM	IF	LM	OM	TM
Capacity						
Cooperation	0.765					
Implementation framework	0.328	0.169				
Legal	0.313	0.216	0.876			
Organisational	0.786	0.590	0.269	0.293		
Technical	0.576	0.429	0.170	0.126	0.699	

Discriminant validity is the last assessment done in the measurement model. This determines that two unrelated constructs are theoretically not connected. Three approaches are generally used to assess discriminant validity. They are Fornell and Larcker's [19] criteria, cross-loadings, and the Heterotrait-Monotrait Ration (HTMT) criterion [9]. However, PLS-SEM recommends using HTMT.

The HTMT criterion estimates the true correlation between two constructs as if they were perfectly reliable. HTMT value above 0.90 suggests a lack of discriminant validity. From Table VI, all constructs in our model score below 0.90, hence the indication of model discriminant validity.

2) Structural Model Assessment

After satisfying all the measurement model requirements, an assessment is conducted on the structure of the model to test the hypothesis of the study. Multicollinearity amongst constructs is assessed using the variance inflation factor (VIF). Higher VIF indicates critical levels of collinearity, with values below 5 being desirable. Table VII shows the VIF values for the constructs in the research model, with the highest being 3.987, indicating good indicator collinearity. Higher VIF indicates critical levels of collinearity, with values below 5 being desirable. Table VII shows the VIF values for the constructs in the research model, with the highest being 3.987, indicating good indicator collinearity.

TABLE VII. VARIANCE INFLATION FACTOR (VIF)

Constructs	VIF
Capacity	3.987
Cooperation	2.422
Legal	1.106
Organisational	2.895
Technical	1.758

Once there are no collinearity issues amongst the indicators, the value of R^2 was computed to determine the in-sample predictive power of the model. R^2 values range from 0 to 1, with higher values closer to 1 indicating better predictability of the structural model. R^2 for this model is 0.710, as indicated in Table VIII, which is closer to the substantial preferred value of 0.75 and greater than the moderate value of 0.5. This indicates that the model predicts by a combined percentage of 71% how legal, technical, organisational, capacity development, and cooperation measures predict the policy implementation framework of the 2020 Cyber Security Act 1038 by financial institutions in Ghana.

TABLE VIII. MODEL FIT WITH R^2

	R^2	Adjusted R^2
Implementation framework	0.686	0.675

The effect size represents the change in the coefficient of determination when a specified construct is omitted from the model. This is measured with f^2, where values of 0.02, 0.15, and 0.35 represent small, medium, and large effects, respectively. Thus, values of less than 0.02 indicate no effect, whilst values above 0.15 indicate significant effects. From

Table 4.8, legal measures have the largest effect size with values of 1.788. Capacity had 0.043 which is substantive. Cooperation and technical measures had medium effects with 0.025 and 0.015 respectively. Organisational had no effect with a value of 0.011 which is below 0.02.

Hair *et al.* [20] recommend a minimum acceptable sample size for bootstrapping to be 1000 samples. However, for more reliability, a sample size of 10000 was chosen using a two-tailed distribution with a bias-corrected and accelerated (BCa) bootstrap method. This produced *t*-values and *p*-values as shown in Table IX.

At the 0.95 significance level, *t*-values above 1.96 show significance, whilst values below show no significance. In that order, legal measures, cooperation measures, and capacity measures are significant. t-values of 1.649 and 1.112 for technical and organisational measures indicate they have no statistical significance in this research model.

TABLE IX. EFFECT SIZE

Constructs	Effect size (f^2)
Capacity	0.043
Cooperation	0.025
Legal	1.788
Organisational	0.011
Technical	0.015

Hair *et al.* [20] recommends *t*-values of at least 196 before a hypothesis can be inferred as supported. Therefore, this model supports three of our hypotheses outlined in Section 3. H_2 and H_3 are rejected based on the t-values. H_1, H_4, and H_5 can be considered viable hypotheses and hence accepted.

TABLE X. CONSTRUCTS SIGNIFICANCE

	Original Sample (O)	Sample Mean (M)	Standard Deviation	T Statistics (|O/STDEV|)	*p*-values		
Legal =>implementation	0.358	0.356	0.024	15.037	0.000	H_1	**Supported**
Technical -> implementation	0.042	0.042	0.025	1.649	0.099	H_2	Not Supported
Organisational -> implementation	-0.045	-0.043	0.04	1.112	0.266	H_3	Not Supported
Capacity -> implementation	0.105	0.105	0.045	2.339	0.019	H_4	**Supported**
Cooperation -> implementation	-0.063	-0.063	0.029	2.154	0.031	H_5	**Supported**

C. Constraints and Enabling factors

All the interviewed participants affirmed their knowledge of the 2020 Cyber Security Act and indicated that their organizations are taking steps to implement it. With regards to the frequency of review of cyber security policies, about 90% of the participants suggested 2 years and must be guided by the frequent changes in the threat landscape in the cyber ecosystem. At the organizational level, it is recommended that policies are reviewed annually, but when new threats or technologies emerge, changes in national or international regulations occur, or internal incidents happen that were not captured in existing policies, they should be reviewed and updated. Tables XI and XII are sample extracts (response) from participants during the interview.

TABLE XI. CONSTRAINTS OF IMPLEMENTING CYBER SCEIRTY ACT IN GHANA

	Sample Extract	Identified Themes
1	*"For the implementation, it's fully done. But it's one thing to implement and another to enforce. Now the question is, are we enforcing all the policies in the act as stated??"*	Policy enforcement
2	*"In my opinion, the cost and resources are the constraints. Cost can be broken down into infrastructure and human resource costs. Resources will be human and tools to be used."*	Financial cost, Limited technical capacity, Human resources
3	*"Lack of awareness on the 2020 Cyber Security Act 1038"*	Lack of awareness
4	*"The understanding of Act 1038 is still not too much by the public and the institutions tasked to implement, simply because the institutions tasked to do so may not be doing its job"*	Lack of understanding of the Act, Ineffective organisations

TABLE XII. ENABLING FACTORS FOR IMPLEMENTATION OF CYBER SECURITY ACT IN GHANA

	Sample Extract	Identified Themes
1	*"The first task is to identify those charged to implement it and those charged to ensure more education. Identification of what has been done so far by these two separate bodies will inform the awareness mechanism to undertake. When people get informed, it empowers them to take proactive and preventive actions"*	Collaboration Awareness
2	*"Training of persons in IT roles to enable them to focus on cyber security issues. Government to give waivers for certain cyber security tools or operations for cyber security service providers"*	Training Government support
3	*"Creation of awareness on the Cyber Security Act amongst stakeholders. Capacity building and knowledge transfer between personnel of stakeholder agencies.*	Collaboration, Awareness creation, Capacity building
4	*"Establish and adopt cyber security standards for education, skills development, risk management, research and development and practitioners."*	Cyber security standards, Skills development, Research

V. DISCUSSION

The ITU's Global Cyber Security Index assessed Ghana's cyber security score as 89.69% in 2021, a significant increase from 32.6% in 2017 [6]. This achievement was celebrated by the CSA and the Ghana Ministry of Communication, as it placed Ghana in the 3rd position as the most cyber-committed country in Africa after Mauritius and Tanzania. The assessment evaluated five key pillars, including legal, technical, organizational, capacity development, and cooperation measures [10]. However, the public financial institutions in Ghana still need to fully comply with the ITU's cyber security index despite Ghana's progress in the cyber space due to the implementation of the Act.

The findings of this study indicate that the public financial institutions in Ghana have sufficient legal measures to implement the 2020 Cyber Security Act 1038, which is a crucial determinant of the model's reliability. Financial institutions in Ghana have appropriate policy and regulatory measures on data protection, unauthorised use of computer systems, and cyber security audit and risk management. However, policies on enforcing cyber security standards, managing online harassment, and mitigating cyber security risks are either non-existent or inadequate, despite public financial institutions in Ghana implementing several policy measures

The study findings indicate that financial institutions in Ghana lack adequate technical capacity to comply with the Cyber Security Act 1038. This means that these institutions do not have sufficient technical measures to implement the Act. Despite these technical limitations, financial institutions in Ghana employ only certified cyber security professionals and procure and use genuine software systems, as the risks and implications of using pirated or fake software are high. This is due to the strict directive from the Bank of Ghana, which enforces regulations that require all financial institutions in Ghana to only employ certified IT managers and chief information security officers.

The study rejects the third hypothesis, which states that public financial institutions in Ghana are organized to implement the 2020 Cyber Security Act 1038. Critical organizational measures that are lacking include the absence of a dedicated cyber security unit, and cyber security policies that are not readily available and disseminated [18]. Additionally, the management of financial institutions in Ghana must be more committed to supporting the implementation of the Act through financial support and any other means possible at the strategic level. The supervisory division of the Bank of Ghana could help ensure proper organization of financial institutions in terms of cyber security implementation and enforcement.

The study has found that the capacity building development initiative by financial institutions in Ghana is satisfactory. However, more needs to be done to increase their capacity building initiatives through investing in cyber security infrastructure, research, and providing security education, training, and awareness. In addition, the study identified constraints in the implementation of the Cyber Security Act, including lack of awareness and training, lack of top management support, policy enforcement challenges, lack of understanding of the Act, and user non-compliance. The study also highlighted cross-cutting themes, including awareness creation and training, policy enforcement, cyber security technical measures and standards, human resource development, management support, and collaboration, which need to be addressed to enable the successful implementation of the Act. It is crucial to provide these enabling factors for the implementation of the 2020 Cyber Security Act 1038. Moreover, CSA should be supported and equipped to perform its mandates while developing the capacities of various CIIs and stakeholders necessary to ensure the Act's successful implementation

VI. Conclusion

Based on the Global Cyber Security Index and the Ghana National Cyber Security Policy and Strategy, a conceptual framework was developed to explore the state of the implementation of cyber security in Ghana. Five key themes were identified, which underpin all cyber security policies and implementation strategies. These are legal, technical, organizational, capacity development, and cooperation measures. Questionnaires were administered and interviews were conducted to collect data. The study found that financial institutions have instituted several policy measures but lack the capacity to implement them. In future, we intend to expand the study by exploring he various cyber security techniques being adopted by the financial institutions in Ghana.

References

[1] D. Thapa and Ø., Saebø, "Exploring the link between ICT and development in the context of developing countries: A literature review" The Electronic Journal of Information Systems in Developing Countries, vol 64, no. 1, pp. 1-15, 2014.

[2] Statistica, "Internetusers in the world 2022". [Retrieved: January 2023] https://rb.gy/7h9ots

[3] M. Hepfer and T.C. Powell, "Make Cybersecurity a Strategic Asset". MIT Sloan Mgt. Review, vol. 63, no. 1, 4pp. 0-45, 2020

[4] V. Lebogang, O. Tabona., and T. Maupong, "Evaluating Cybersecurity Strategies in Africa". In Cybersecurity Capabilities in Developing Nations and Its Impact on Global Security, pp. 1-19, 2022.

[5] R. Sabillon, V. Cavaller and J. Cano, "National cyber security strategies: global trends in cyberspace. International Journal of Computer Science and Software Eng. Vo. 5, no.5, p. 67, 2016.

[6] O. Longe, O. Ngwa, F. Wada, V. Mbarika, and L. Kv asny,"Criminal Use of Informationand Communication Technologies in Sub-Saharan Africa: Trends, Concerns andPerspectives". Journal of Information Technology Impact, vol 9, no. 3, pp.155-165, 2009.

[7] Paliament of Ghana, "Cyber Security Act 2020". [Retrieved: January 2023] available at https://rb.gy/al3oky

[8] GNCSP. "Ghana National cyber security policy and strategy" [Retrieved: January 2023], available at https://rb.gy/7u9lfj

[9] J.F Hair, J.J Risher, M. Sarstedt, C.M, Ringle "When to use and how to report the results of PLS-SEM". European business review. Vol. 3, no. 1, pp. 1-24, 2019

[10] ITU (2015), "Global security index". [Retrieved: January 2023] https://www.itu.int/en/action/cybersecurity/Pages/gca.aspx

[11] M. Kaur, "Cyber Security Challenges in the Latest Technology". In Proceedings of Third International Conference on Communication, Computing and Electronics Systems, pp. 655-671, 2022.

[12] J.F Hair, G.T.M. Hult, C.M Ringle, M. Sarstedt, "A primer on partial least squares structural equation modeling (PLS-SEM)".Sage publications, New York, 2021.

[13] J. Mayoh, and A.J. Onwuegbuzie, "Toward a conceptualization of mixed methods phenomenological research". Journal of mixed methods research, vol. 9 no. 1, pp. 91-107, 2021.

[14] J.L Myers, A.D Well, and R.F Jr, "Research design and statistical analysis" 3rd ed, Routledge, 2013.

[15] E. Dubois and U. Tatar "Data analysis in research: Why data, types of data, data analysis in qualitative and quantitative research. QuestionPro. [Retrieved: January 2023] at https://rb.gy/apfphh

[16] K.K.K Wong, "Mastering Partial Least Squares Structural Equation modelling " Universe: Bloomington. IN, USA, pp. 1-184, 2019.

[17] Jr., J. F., Hult, G. T., Ringle, C. M., Sarstedt, M., Danks, N. P., and Ray, S. "Partial least squares structural equation modelling (PLS-SEM) using R: A workbook" no. 1, pp. XIV. 197. 2021
[18] Bank of Ghana (2018). Cyber and Information security directives. [Retrieved: January 2023], https://rb.gy/ylvoz
[19] C. Fornell and D.F, larcker, " Evaluating structural equation models with unobservable variables and measurement error". Journal of Marketing Research, vol 18, no. 1, pp. 39–50, 1981.
[20] J., Hair, C, Ringle, and m. Sarstedt, M., "PLS-SEM: Indeed a Silver Bullet", Journal of Marketing Theory and Practice, no. 19, pp. 139-151, 2011.

Long-Term Risks of IoT Devices: The Case of the Smart Fridge

Erik Buchmann[a,b]

[a] Dept. of Computer Science, Leipzig University, Germany
[b] Center for Scalable Data Analytics and Artificial Intelligence Dresden/Leipzig, Germany
Email: buchmann@informatik.uni-leipzig.de

***Abstract*—Replacing conventional devices with smart ones has many advantages, e.g., a seamless integration of physical objects into the user's digital environment or improved modes of use. However, if a conventional device is replaced by a smart device, its IT components can cause risks, that shorten the life of the device. Such risks stem from different life cycles of embedded soft- and hardware, libraries and protocols used, and the IT ecosystem required. This is problematic, because many conventional household appliances, say, a fridge or TV, have a much longer life span than typical IT equipment. In this paper, we use a systematic approach to identify long-term risks for the operational life span of a smart fridge. In particular, we identify 8 different use cases of three typical smart fridges, e.g., cooling or managing "best before" dates. We model the IT ecosystem needed to run these use cases, and we inspect each asset in this ecosystem for potential long-term risks. We found that even cooling, the most basic use case, is at risk in the long run. This is because the setting cooling parameters may depend on parts of the IT ecosystem that are not under the user's control. On the other hand, we did not find any risk that may lead to harm of the category "threatening". Our findings on the smart fridge can be generalized to other smart devices easily.**

***Keywords*—Internet of Things; Security; Risk Management**

I. INTRODUCTION

Advances in hard- and software have led to the trend to add sensors, computational resources and communication interfaces to traditional consumer products, and to connect them over the Internet to cloud services where an artificial intelligence approach interprets voice commands or enhance user experience. Together, such smart devices form the Internet of Things (IoT) [1]. In many cases, smart devices stem from non-smart predecessors. For example, a modern smart refrigerator looks and feels much like a classic non-smart refrigerator with some extras, e.g., remote control and expiration management for perishable foods.

Smart devices allow consumers to create smart homes with devices that can be controlled remotely via smartphone, adapt to the user's habits, and provide convenient services locally or on the Internet. However, media provide evidence that smart devices might come with operational risks that occur well after the time of purchase. With a familiar non-smart device in mind, customers may not expect risks like Examples 1-3, when choosing a smart device.

Example 1: *The software of a smart device may have an operational life-span that is much shorter than the life-span of its hardware [2]. For example, without regular functional and security updates, a smart TV soon becomes useless [3].*

Example 2: *Smart devices may be tied to a cloud service. For example, after a third-party service provider ceased its business, tens of thousands smart Internet radios became non-functional [4] without warning in advance.*

Example 3: *Changes in the legislation may prohibit the use of smart devices after years of operation. In Germany, for example, a child's smart toy [5] has been forbidden as a spying tool, three years after it had been introduced to the market, because it was not visible that the toy sends voice recordings into the cloud.*

In order to make smart devices accessible for risk management, a comprehensive catalog of potential risks is required. It is challenging to find a research method that delivers such a catalog. For example, the results of a study [6] depend on the insights of the study participants.

In this paper, we use smart fridges as a use case to compile a comprehensive set of long-term risks that are (a) specific for the smart fridge, i.e., do not exist for conventional fridges, and (b) may materialize years after the fridge has been purchased. We define our problem statement as follows:

Which specific risks for the continued long-term use of a smart fridge may appear after purchase, but cannot be expected from a conventional fridge?

We call a fridge a "smart fridge", if it contains computational capabilities and data links, which are not essential for the primary function "cooling food products". By "long-term", we refer to an operational life of >10 years, which can be expected from a fridge's hardware [7]. Intuitively, this may be the expectation of a customer replacing a broken fridge.

In this paper, we adapt our research method from [8] to methodically derive such long-term risks for a smart fridge in a domestic environment. We have identified *compliance risks* resulting from changing local, national or international rules, *economic risks* from future business decisions of the organizations involved, and *operational risks* considering the technical perspective of operating a smart fridge together with its IT ecosystem for more than 10 years. Due to our methodical approach, we consider our set of risks to be complete for this application scenario. We think that it can be easily adapted to similar scenarios.

The paper is structured as follows: In Section II, we briefly review related work. In Section III, we sketch our approach to identify long-term risks of smart fridges. In Section IV, we use this approach to obtain our set of risks. Section V concludes.

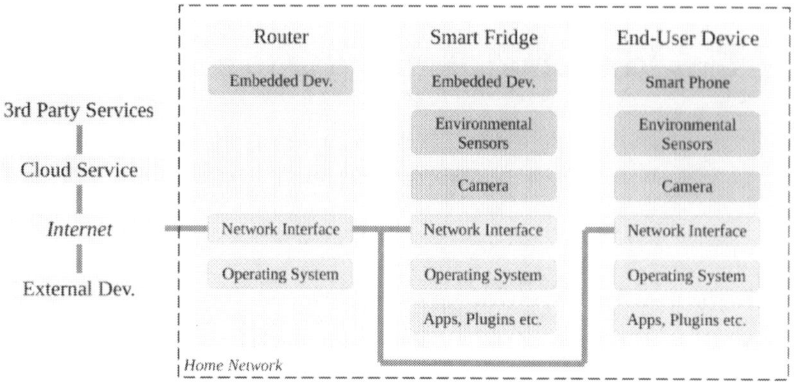

Figure 1. IT Architecture

II. Related Work

This section summarizes methods, standards and findings related to our work. **Design science research** [9] is a method to design an artefact from a knowledge base, and evaluate and improve it in several rounds. Each round is divided into three cycles: The *relevance cycle* specifies and refines the use cases needed to construct the artefact and evaluate its applicability. The *rigor cycle* builds a knowledge base from literature and experience that is needed to evaluate the novelty and the research contribution of the artefact. The central *design cycle* iterates between building and evaluating the artefact, based on information from the other cycles.

The **BSI-Standard 200-3** [10] is based on IT-Grundschutz. It defines a process that allows organizations to assess their information security risks. In particular, the standard describes how to identify, classify, consolidate, assess and treat risks. Our concern is risk identification. In this respect, the standard distinguishes risks that arise from *elementary threats*, e.g., fire, theft, misconfiguration or manipulation, and *specific threats* from specific use cases. The risk identification starts with the modelling of the use cases. The risk catalog is then compiled from the consolidated risks of the individual IT assets, which are part of the model.

Advances in technology call for **risk analyses** before adoption. However, risk analyses typically use a descriptive research approach, focus on the current situation and/or have a narrow perspective, e.g., on current IT security or return on investment. For example, [11] reviews vulnerabilities of smart devices in the consumer market. The risk assessment approach in [12] considers the management of risk over the past two years, but does not project into the future, e.g., when security breaches remain untreated for a discontinued product. A study [6] provides a holistic view on future IoT risks, but a standardized questionnaire cannot provide a complete overview on future risks. In consequence, existing approaches that deal with IoT risks during the operational life of the device [13] [14] do not consider that vendors may loose interest in supporting discontinued products, or that it will be hard to find experts to maintain outdated technology. [2] uses threat models to assess risks due to discontinued services, breaking updates, trade conflicts, etc., but it remains unclear if this risk assessment is exhaustive for the devices in question. In [8], we have defined a research method to identify long-term risks that are specific for smart devices. Because this method is fundamental for our paper, we will explain it in more detail in the next section.

The **long-term preservation of digital goods** has been extensively discussed [15] in the past years. The risks for digital content [16] overlap with the risks of using an outdated smart device in a modern environment. Examples are media obsolescence and format obsolescence [16], i.e., the digital object cannot be read with current devices due new media or new formats. Security properties have been established with protocols that are insecure now [17]. Digital objects, such as dynamic web pages [18] or computer games [19], require a complex execution environment.

III. How to Identify Long-Term IoT Risks

In this section, we briefly describe our research method, which we have developed in [8]. Our method adapts BSI-Standard 200-3 [10] so that it creates the knowledge base and designs a risk catalog that fits into relevance and design cycle of Design Science Research [9]. We use research literature to foster the rigor cycle.

For this paper, we have extended two aspects of [8]: We explicitly refer to an operational scenario (in our case: a domestic environment) to assess the extent of potential harms and damages. Furthermore, we do not add assets to our infrastructure model that do not add specific risks for the smart device in question, e.g., the Internet router or the electricity supplier. In particular, we use the following steps:

1) Select typical devices and identify the use cases for these devices in a given scenario. Model its IT infrastructure.
2) Determine under which conditions each asset in this infrastructure operates as intended by the use cases.
3) Append this condition to the risk set, if it is not present at purchase and doesn't exist for non-smart devices.
4) Assess the harm the risks could cause, and consolidate risks that are identical for multiple assets.
5) Back up each individual risk by literature.

IV. Long-term Risks of a Smart Fridge

In this section, we apply our research method from Section III to identify a comprehensive set of long-term risks associated with smart fridges.

Operational scenario: We base our analysis on a domestic environment, where the fridge stores perishable food that needs cooling and has a limited economic value. The user of the fridge values the user experience more than privacy and likes to use all technical possibilities of the digital services offered by the smart fridge. The user can be expected to detect spoiled food, but does not possess the IT-security knowledge needed to detect cyber attacks on the smart fridge. Figure 1 illustrates the IT architecture for this scenario.

A. Device Selection and Use Cases

According to Step 1 of our research method, we select three typical devices from the category "Smart Fridge":

1) Bosch KGN36HI32
2) Samsung RF27T5501SG
3) LG GSX960NEAZ

The Bosch KGN36HI32 can be controlled via the Bosch Home Connect platform, which connects to Amazon Alexa and other voice assistants and sends temperature alarms to the user's smartphone. It is equipped with internal cameras, that monitor the cooled food products. The Samsung RF27T5501SG provides similar technical features as the Bosch fridge, but uses the Samsung product family: It contains a Samsung Family Hub and connects to a voice assistant called Bixby. In addition, it provides a large LCD screen with apps and Internet access via WLAN, and an ice dispenser. The LG GSX960NEAZ provides the smallest set of smart features: It only controls fridge parameters and functions, such as defrost and alerts, via LG smartphone app. But it does not contain cameras, smart home hubs or LCD screens.

TABLE I. Categories of Use Cases

Id	*Name*	*Description*
U1	Cooling	Storing and cooling food products.
U2	Monitoring	Monitoring the food storage via camera.
U3	Management	Managing food expiration and shopping lists.
U4	Shopping	Replenish food storage.
U5	Multimedia	Playing music, TV streams, Internet access.
U6	Remote	Remote control of cooling and alarms.
U7	Apps	Other apps, e.g., for searching wine temperatures.
U8	Updates	Functional upgrades or security updates.

To obtain typical use cases for smart fridges, we have browsed the manuals and web pages of our selected devices. Table I lists all use cases we have identified. **Cooling** (U1) is the traditional use of a fridge. **Monitoring** (U2), **management** (U3), **shopping** (U4) and **remote control** (U6) refer to typical domestic requirements, which are now enhanced by digital services. Smartphone apps control cooling parameters and various alarms (opening, temperature, humidity), look inside the fridge via cameras, and might also identify food products that are used up or are close to its expiration date. If the smart fridge is part of a larger smart-home solution, it typically serves as a **multimedia** (U5) hub to deliver audio and video streams to connected devices. Some smart fridges allow **further apps** (U7), e.g., to manage recipes, to search for optimal wine temperatures or to browse the Internet. **Updates** (U8) are important to maintain the security and functionality of the smart fridge during its operational life.

B. IT Infrastructure Model

TABLE II. Categories of Devices

Id	*Name*	*Description*
A1	Smart Fridge	The smart fridge.
A2	End-User Dev.	Smartphone (WLAN), TV, smart speaker, etc.
A3	Cloud	Digital fridge services on the Internet.
A4	3rd Party Serv.	Digital smart home services on the Internet.
A5	External Dev.	Smartphone (LTE) or tablet (LTE).

Table II lists all categories of devices or appliances needed to run the use-cases U1-U8. The **smart fridge** (A1) contains an embedded computing device with network interface and operating system. It may or may not also contain further plugins and apps, e.g. a web browser. Some smart fridges are equipped with internal cameras that monitor the stored food products. Any smart fridge we are aware makes use of sensors to monitor parameters, such as temperature and moisture. Both **end-user device** (A2) and **external device** (A5) are used to control any smart, digital service the fridge offers. Respective devices include laptops, smartphones, tablets, smart TVs or smart speakers. The difference between A2 and A5 is that the external device connects via LTE, i.e., it uses a network connection that leaves the home WLAN. Thus, we need to model it separately. A3 refers to a **cloud service** that is bundled with the smart fridge, and provides services tailored to the fridge. For example, Bosch KGN36HI32 connects to Bosch Home Connect. In contrast, A4 means any other **3rd-party service**, e.g., a smart-home system, a voice assistant or a content-delivery network from a third-party cloud. Since our focus is on the smart fridge, we leave aside the router.

TABLE III. Categories of Data

Id	*Name*	*Description*
D1	Sensor data	Video, audio, temperature, power consumption.
D2	App data	Data from apps installed on the smart fridge.
D3	Metadata	Timestamps, soft- and hardware versions.
D4	Configuration	Parameters, credentials, certificates.
D5	Telemetry	Device behavior, log information.
D6	Op. System	Software libs, updates, operating system data.

Use cases U1-U8 require the smart fridge to manage and share 6 categories of data with devices A1-A5, as shown in Table III. **Sensor data** (D1) includes any information delivered by internal sensors of the fridge, e.g., video streams from an internal camera or the temperature in the wine compartment. **App data** (D2) refers to data managed by the various kinds of apps executed on the smart fridge. Examples are the user's shopping lists, multimedia data from external parties or expiration dates. **Metadata** (D3) is any information produced by the operation of smart services. Examples include version numbers, timestamps or patch levels of software libraries. **Configuration** (D4) data stores parameters about how the use cases should work. This means cooling parameters as well as WLAN credentials or HTTPS certificates. **Telemetry** (D5) means any information that is typically part of the log file of the smart fridge, e.g., internal errors, defrost times, power outage, and the like. **Operating System** (D6) refers to the program code of the operating system and its apps, updates, patches, libraries, etc.

TABLE IV. CATEGORIES OF ORGANIZATIONS

Id	*Name*	*Description*
O1	User	The user of the smart fridge.
O2	Vendor	The manufacturer of the smart fridge.
O3	Cloud Provider	The operator of the cloud service.
O4	3rd Party Provider	External cloud service providers.
O5	Other 3rd Parties	Other services.

The devices are operated by different parties, as shown in Table IV. Since our problem definition focuses on specific risks for a smart fridge, we leave aside the parties that might cause generic risks. Such parties are the Internet provider, the LTE provider or the electricity supplier. Large companies, such as LG, have their own cloud infrastructure and cloud services, like voice assistants used by the smart fridge. Thus, O2 and O3 can be the same organization.

TABLE V. CATEGORIES OF NETWORK CONNECTIONS

Id	*Devices*	*Int.*	*Pers.*	*Description*
C1	A1-A2	✓	✓	smart fridge – end-user device
C2	A2-A3	✗	✓	end-user device – cloud
C3	A1-A3	✗	✓	smart fridge – cloud
C4	A3-A4	✗	✓	cloud – 3rd party cloud
C5	A1-A5	✗	✓	smart fridge – external device

Table V contains all categories of network connections we need to consider. Note that all connections are bi-directional. Column "Int." indicates that a connection transfers data within the home WLAN. "Pers." means that a connection might transfer data related to the activities or habits of a person.

TABLE VI. ASSET MATRIX

U. C.	*Data*	*Devices*	*Connections*	*Orga.*
U1	D1, D3-D5	A1		O1
U2	D1-D4	A1, A2, A5	C1, C5	O1
U3	D2-D4	A1-A3, A5	C1-C3, C5	O1, O3
U4	D2-D4	A1, A2, A4, A5	C1, C4, C5	O1, O4
U5	D2-D4	A1-A5	C1-C5	O1, O4
U6	D1-D5	A1-A3, A5	C1-C3, C5	O1, O3
U7	D1-D5	A1-A5	C1-C5	O1, O3-O5
U8	D2-D6	A1, A3	C3	O2

After having defined the categories of use cases, devices, data, organizations and network connections we need to consider, we can define an asset matrix (cf. Table VI). The asset matrix tells which use case is tied to which IT asset. U1 (Cooling) is the only use case that does not need network connections, other devices or other organizations. All other use cases depend on an operational IT ecosystem.

C. Potential Harms and Damages

Table I allows us to devise four categories of potential harm, as shown in Table VII. The categories are in line with [20]. Potentially, a smart fridge may produce threatening physical or financial damages, e.g., from spoiled food or a violation of legal regulations. Negligible harm could be a brief interruption or malfunction of digital or cooling services.

TABLE VII. CATEGORIES OF POTENTIAL HARM

Category	*Examples*
negligible	Food spoils a bit earlier, digital services are unavailable for a short time, isolated false alarms.
limited	Fridge contents spoils, services are unavailable for some time, many false alarms.
substantial	Permanent unavailability of digital services or cooling results in a total economic loss, privacy issues.
threatening	High fines from violation of the law results in private insolvency, severe sickness from food poisoning.

From Table VII we can derive the protection needs of the data. In Table VIII, we have analyzed if an interruption, interception, modification or fabrication of data has an impact on integrity, availability or confidentiality. If this impact can produce negligible or limited harm, the protection need is normal. If it can be substantial, the protection need is high. If the harm can be threatening, the protection need is very high.

TABLE VIII. PROTECTION NEEDS

Data	*Integrity*	*Availability*	*Confidentiality*
D1	normal	normal	high
D2	normal	normal	high
D3	normal	normal	high
D4	high	high	high
D5	normal	normal	high
D6	high	high	high

D1–D5 might allow to infer personal information, e.g., eating habits, preferred foods, the daily routine or if the user is sick or on vacation. Thus, D1–D5 have "high" protection needs for confidentiality. The security of the user's network and the functionality of the fridge depend on D4 and D6. A misconfiguration, a disclosure of passwords, a manipulated OS update or an attacker knowing the patch-level of the software might result in a substantial harm (cf. Table VII). Thus, D4 and D6 have the protection need "high" for all three dimensions. In our domestic setting, a threatening harm is highly improbable, and we do not assign the protection need "very high". This may be different in other scenarios, e.g., if a hospital uses the smart fridge to cool medications.

The protection needs are inherited from the data to each IT asset managing the data, as listed in the asset matrix Table VI. The maximum principle requires that an asset is assigned with the highest protection need of all data it uses. For example, the vendor's cloud (A3) is part of the use case "Update" (U8), which includes data of the operation system (D6) with the protection need "high" for the protection dimensions integrity, availability and confidentiality. Thus, even if A3 handles less sensible data (D1 and D2), the protection need of A3 is "high" for each protection dimension.

From the asset matrix it follows that *any* device, network connection and organization need to maintain a "high" level of protection for each dimension, because either D4 or D6 is part of any use case. As consequence from the asset matrix,

TABLE IX. LONG-TERM COMPLIANCE RISKS

Risk	*Orga.*	*Devices*	*Connections*	*Description*
Privacy	O2-O5	A2-A5	C2-C5	Changing legislation, new codes of conduct, etc. impose limitations on the exchange of personal data with certain countries or parties [21].
Global Rules	O2-O5	A2-A4	C2-C4	New trade restrictions, sanctions, technology bans etc. restrict the use of an asset from certain countries or parties [22].
Local Rules	O1-O5	A1-A5	C1-C5	Local regulations, e.g., from environmental protection, consumer protection or electromagnetic compatibility, restrict the use of an asset [23].
Expiration	O2-O5	A1-A5	C1-C5	Disagreements to common compliance standards, expired certifications or approvals, non-renewed audits, etc., render the involved asset untrusted [24].
Concealment	O1-O5	A1-A5	C1-C5	Unknown characteristics at time of purchase disallow the further use of an asset, e.g., if it turns out that a build-in camera falls under espionage acts [5].

TABLE X. LONG-TERM ECONOMIC RISKS

Risk	*Orga.*	*Devices*	*Connections*	*Description*
Degradation	O2-O5	A3, A4	C2-C4	The service quality of an asset might be reduced, e.g., to nudge customers into new services by delaying updates or reducing performance of old services [25].
Licensing	O2-O5	A1, A3, A4	C2-C4	The revenue model might change. For example, an organization might switch its services to a pay-per-use model for an asset [26].
Discontinuation	O2-O5	A3, A4	C2-C5	One of the parties involved discontinues its service or makes it unattractive to use it from an economic point of view [27].
Liabilities	O2-O5	A3, A4	C2-C5	One of the parties involved discontinues its business, and its contractual liabilities become void at once [28].

TABLE XI. LONG-TERM OPERATIONAL RISKS

Risk	*Orga.*	*Devices*	*Connections*	*Description*
Inflexibility	O1-O5	A1-A5	C1-C5	Due to missing functional updates, it becomes challenging to connect an asset to recent services or devices [29].
Unreliability	O2-O5	A1-A5	C1-C5	The service level in terms of reliability, throughput, etc. of the asset degrades, e.g., due to reduced support for legacy products [30].
Unmaintainability	O2	A1	C1, C3, C5	Due to the use of outdated interfaces and closed-source components it becomes difficult to find manuals, experts or spare parts to that maintain the asset [31].
Insecurity	O2	A1	C1, C3, C5	Without security updates and by using out-of-date security protocols, the asset cannot be operated any more [30].
Defectiveness	O2	A1	C1, C3, C5	Modernizations in the IT ecosystem make technical debts of an asset visible, e.g., if a network protocol uses bits that were reserved for future use [32].

it is problematic to use a smart fridge as a multimedia hub in a smart home as well. Because the fridge runs services with "high" protection needs, the much less sensitive media-playback service must be secured at level "high" as well.

D. Long-Term Risks

After having identified the potential harms and the assets in our IT ecosystem that need special protection, we can compile IT-security risks. In order to obtain a comprehensive set of risks, we inspect each asset (organization, device, connection) in isolation, and we look for reasons why, at some point in the future, the asset in question will no longer operate as it did at the time of purchase. Recall that we are specifically interested in long-term risks of the smart fridge. Thus, in line with Step 3 of our research method, we filter out any potential risk that (a) is apparent at the time of purchase, or (b) is identical for a traditional fridge and a smart fridge. For example, we do not consider risks, such as the smart fridge is delivered with a pre-installed virus in its operating system, or the cooling unit fails after some time.

The resulting set of risks is long and repetitive, because some risks materialize across different assets. For example, licensing risks due to changing revenue models can affect many assets and network connections at some time in the future, and occur at multiple organizations. For this reason, we need Step 4 of our research method to consolidate risks.

Tables IX-XI show our consolidated set of long-term risks for 8 use cases for smart fridges. To our surprise, many of those risks are identical to the risks, which we had exemplarily identified for a single artefact (the network connection between a smart device and a cloud server) in [8]. This confirms the reproducibility of our research method.

We have structured our set of risks into three groups: **Long-term compliance risks** are produced by changing local, national or international rules and standards. Risks from this group mean that using the smart fridge may violate regulatory requirements in the future, even if it has fully complied with them at the time of purchase. **Long-term economic risks** are the result of future business decisions of the organizations involved. Seven of the identified use cases require a complex IT ecosystem, as shown in our asset matrix (Table VI). If an organization ceases operation or moves to a different revenue model in the future, the remaining IT ecosystem may no longer able to support all use cases in an economic manner. This also includes a pay-per-security-update model. Finally, **long-term operational risks** consider the technical perspective of operating a smart fridge together with its IT ecosystem for more than 10 years. Operational risks include technical challenges when trying to connect an outdated device to a new one, and maintenance issues due to missing experts and spare parts for the IT ecosystem needed.

The tables only specify risks that impede a smart fridge, even if the same risk may be also associated with other devices in our IT ecosystem. For example, risk "Unmaintainability" is listed for device A1 (the fridge itself) and organization O2 (the fridge's vendor), although the same risk exists for any other IT asset that is used for a decade or more.

Note that even "cooling" (U1), the most basic use case, is at risk in the long run. A smart fridge may have a reduced control panel. Such fridges depend on the use case "remote" (U6), which needs an Internet connection to the vendor's cloud and a smartphone app. For example, the Samsung RF27T5501SG requires the user to download the "SmartThings" app and register for the Samsung cloud with a personalized account.

V. CONCLUSION

When non-smart devices are replaced by smart ones, the integrated IT components generate new risks, that may limit the operational life-span of the smart device unexpectedly. Such risks originate from different life cycles of digital and physical objects, from changing legislation, from future business decisions by the parties involved and from the technical complexity of the IT ecosystem needed.

In this paper, we have compiled a catalog of long-term risks for smart fridges. Our catalog consists of risks, which might materialize years after the purchase. The risks are specific to the smart device, i.e., we have omitted any traditional risk that also exists for conventional fridges. Because we have used a well-structured research method, we think that our risk catalog is exhaustive for compliance risks, economic risks and operational risks. Our risk catalog can be adapted to many use cases and smart devices that use a similar IT architecture.

ACKNOWLEDGMENT

We would like to thank Badr Aldin Saada for his outstanding help and support with our risk analysis.

REFERENCES

[1] L. Atzori, A. Iera, and G. Morabito, "The internet of things: A survey," *Computer networks*, vol. 54, no. 15, pp. 2787–2805, 2010.

[2] P. Zdankin, M. Waltereit, V. Matkovic, and T. Weis, "Towards Longevity of Smart Home Systems," in *International Conference on Pervasive Computing and Communications Workshops*, 2020, pp. 1–6.

[3] B. Schoon, "Android tv needs better standards for long-term updates and support," https://9to5google.com/2019/08/29/android-tv-long-term-updates-support/, 2019, retrieved: March, 2023.

[4] Frontier Nuvola Support, "Why did the service change on the 7th may 2019?" https://srsupport.frontier-nuvola.net/portal/en/kb/articles/service-change, 2019, retrieved: 2020-06-10.

[5] V. Gabrielle, "It sees you when you're sleeping: A clash of privacy and play," https://www.governing.com/security/it-sees-you-when-youre-sleeping-a-clash-of-privacy-and-play, 2022, retrieved: March, 2023.

[6] L. M. Tanczer, I. Steenmans, M. Elsden, J. Blackstock, and M. Carr, "Emerging risks in the iot ecosystem: Who's afraid of the big bad smart fridge?" in *Living in the Internet of Things: Cybersecurity of the IoT-2018*, 2018, pp. 1–9.

[7] Statista, "Average life expectancy of major household appliances in 2011 and 2022," https://www.statista.com/statistics/220020/average-life-expectancy-of-major-household-appliances, 2023, retrieved: March, 2023.

[8] E. Buchmann and A. Hartmann, "Identifying long-term risks of the internet of things," in *14th International Conference on Mobile Ubiquitous Computing, Systems, Services and Technologies (UBICOMM'20)*, 2020.

[9] A. Hevner and S. Chatterjee, "Design science research in information systems," in *Design research in information systems*. Springer, 2010, pp. 9–22.

[10] Bundesamt für Sicherheit in der Informationstechnik, "BSI Standard 200-3: Risk Analysis based on IT Grundschutz," *https://www.bsi.bund.de*, 2017, retrieved: March, 2023.

[11] T. Alladi, V. Chamola, B. Sikdar, and K.-K. R. Choo, "Consumer iot: Security vulnerability case studies and solutions," *IEEE Consumer Electronics Magazine*, vol. 9, no. 2, pp. 17–25, 2020.

[12] M. Aydos, Y. Vural, and A. Tekerek, "Assessing risks and threats with layered approach to internet of things security," *Measurement and Control*, vol. 52, no. 5-6, pp. 338–353, 2019.

[13] O. Garcia-Morchon, R. Rietman, S. Sharma, L. Tolhuizen, and J. L. Torre-Arce, "A comprehensive and lightweight security architecture to secure the IoT throughout the lifecycle of a device based on HIMMO," in *Symposium on Algorithms and Experiments for Wireless Sensor Networks*, 2015, pp. 112–128.

[14] J. L. Hernández-Ramos, J. B. Bernabé, and A. Skarmeta, "Army: architecture for a secure and privacy-aware lifecycle of smart objects in the internet of my things," *IEEE Communications Magazine*, vol. 54, no. 9, pp. 28–35, 2016.

[15] Digital Preservation Coalition, "Digital preservation handbook," https://www.dpconline.org/handbook, 2015, retrieved: March, 2023.

[16] S. Vermaaten, B. Lavoie, and P. Caplan, "Identifying threats to successful digital preservation: the spot model for risk assessment," *D-lib Magazine*, vol. 18, no. 9/10, pp. 1–21, 2012.

[17] H. M. Gladney, "Trustworthy 100-year digital objects: Evidence after every witness is dead," *ACM Transactions on Information Systems (TOIS)*, vol. 22, no. 3, pp. 406–436, 2004.

[18] G. Truman, "Web archiving environmental scan: Harvard library report," *Digital Access to Scholarship at Harvard*, 2016.

[19] J. Andersen, "Where games go to sleep: the game preservation crisis," https://www.gamedeveloper.com/business/where-games-go-to-sleep-the-game-preservation-crisis-part-1, 2011, retrieved: March, 2023.

[20] Bundesamt für Sicherheit in der Informationstechnik, "BSI-Standard 200-2, IT-Grundschutz Methodology," https://www.bsi.bund.de, 2017, retrieved: March, 2023.

[21] K. McCullagh, "Brexit: potential trade and data implications for digital and fintech industries," *International Data Privacy Law*, vol. 7, no. 1, p. 3, 2017.

[22] C. Ziye and L. Bin, "China-US High-Tech Competition, Trade Conflict and Development Rights," *China Economist*, vol. 15, no. 5, pp. 66–73, 2020.

[23] Council of the European Union, "Directive 2012/27/EU of the European Parliament and of the Council on energy efficiency, amending Directives 2009/125/EC and 2010/30/EU and repealing Directives 2004/8/EC and 2006/32/EC," Document 02012L0027-20210101, 2021.

[24] Y. T. Mak, S. Carr, and J. Needham, "Differences in strategy, quality management practices and performance reporting systems between ISO accredited and non-ISO accredited companies," *Management Accounting Research*, vol. 8, no. 4, pp. 383–403, 1996.

[25] D. A. Lyons, "Net neutrality and nondiscrimination norms in telecommunications," *Arizona Law Review*, vol. 54, p. 1029, 2013.

[26] M. A. Cusumano, "The changing software business: Moving from products to services," *Computer*, vol. 41, no. 1, pp. 20–27, 2008.

[27] M. A. Lemley and T. Simcoe, "How essential are standard-essential patents," *Cornell Law Review*, vol. 104, p. 607, 2018.

[28] A. Schwartz, "Products liability, corporate structure, and bankruptcy: toxic substances and the remote risk relationship," *Journal of Legal Studies*, vol. 14, no. 3, pp. 689–736, 1985.

[29] P. Mutchler, Y. Safaei, A. Doupé, and J. Mitchell, "Target fragmentation in android apps," in *IEEE Security and Privacy Workshops*. IEEE, 2016, pp. 204–213.

[30] B. Ford, "Icebergs in the clouds: the other risks of cloud computing," in *Hot Topics in Cloud Computing*, 2012, pp. 2–2.

[31] L. M. D. Ferreira, A. Arantes, and C. Silva, "Discontinued products," in *Conference on Operations Research and Enterprise Systems*, 2017, pp. 210–223.

[32] P. Kruchten, R. L. Nord, and I. Ozkaya, "Technical debt: From metaphor to theory and practice," *IEEE Software*, vol. 29, no. 6, pp. 18–21, 2012.

AI Philosophy: Sources of Legitimacy to Analyze Artificial Intelligence

Olga Gil
Instituto Complutense de Ciencias de la Administración
Departamento de Historia, Teorías y Geografía Políticas
Facultad de Ciencias Políticas y Sociología
Universidad Complutense de Madrid
Madrid
olgagil@ucm.es

Abstract—**The following pages aim to reflect upon how to analyze the governance of artificial intelligence in a comparative perspective. In doing so, a dashboard is developed for the analysis and for eventual comparisons between democratic and non democratic regimes. The Gil dashboard of legitimacy would allow us to assess key features that determine the governance model for artificial intelligence at the national level, for local governments and other participant actors. The framework also allows us to appraise aims of the governance strategy, and what aims are left aside. The work opens windows to discuss 1) the complex reality of AI command and control 2) uncertainties about future society and the polity against AI development and 3) cultural values enshrined in countries' AI development. The theoretical framework could be of use to advance case studies globally, and comparative endeavors.**

Keywords- Artificial intelligence; governance; philosophy; ethics; political theory

I. Introduction

This work aims to present a general framework to analyze artificial intelligence (AI), and to discuss legitimacy and governance from political theory as a stream of philosophy. As such, the work addresses questions related to command and control, that are at the base of political and social power and of technical engineering in global societies. In section two, the methodology is introduced. In the third section, the theoretical framework follows. This theoretical framework is based on the sources of legitimacy to analyze artificial intelligence. Here we are bringing to the fore political theory to address a contemporary problem. This part of the work presents an eight dimensional view of sources of legitimacy, based on the works by Max Weber and Craig Mathesson [6][7]. In the fourth section, method as source of change and legitimacy the Gil dashboard on legitimacy are presented. The Dashboard has been developed in a wider context that is not addressed in this short article. The wider context aims to compare the AI regulatory framework of China, the European Union and the United States [1]-[5], which is the endeavor the author is currently devoted to in the draft of a book. The selection of cases, the European Union, the United States and China has been made by their relevance for the development of AI globally today. The case of China has been included because as a political scientist doing comparative politics, the fine line of including most different cases is very important to know better the most equal cases, such as the United States and the European Union, both with democratic components. Today we focus on the theoretical dashboard that has been developed to make the comparisons. In the fifth and last section conclusions are presented, followed by acknowledgments

II. Methodology

The methodology of the general work –the book that the author is writing about artificial intelligence- includes a discussion about the objective of the work, definitions from different perspectives, and questions related to the social basis of knowledge. Additionally, it includes the research approach to the selection of articles reviewed for the work tackled. Finally, the work includes a theoretical framework allowing for a comparison of the three cases, and eventually, a bigger number of cases. For the purpose of comparison of the three main cases in the book of reference, the selection of works started by a search in scopus with the terms artificial intelligence AND China in 2020, 2021, 2022. This brought about 776 works. The selection was further refined under the social sciences category, with 170 documents published matching the query. These works were reviewed looking for governance and legitimacy as topics for retrieval and further work, identifying 37 source articles. Once first relevant works were identified, the reference list of these works became a main source of materials, whether those were included in the scopus database or not, as detailed knowledge became crucial to build up the study. Google scholar was also utilized, searching for the first 10 works on artificial intelligence and social sciences, the 10 most cited works, and the ten most recent ones. These works were reviewed searching for interesting insights. Proquest database has also been consulted, with the query artificial intelligence in the Financial Times newspaper. Specific articles on the query were of value to identify authors with new ideas on artificial intelligence nowadays and how AI affects governance. As a result, these searches brought about information from comparative reports with general information on the United States [1], the work on Europe [2][3], and on China and China local AI ecosystems [4][5] –which I focus on for the purpose of this brief paper.

This research and discussion have been pursued without the aid of artificial intelligences or data bases in the process of ideas. Research and discussion are the result of a human mind. There is no use of any big data software, organic life engineering, or cyborg aid. Thus, at this stage, the results of the work are solely the responsibility of a human author´s mind. At a future stage, it could be explored whether there are interesting possibilities from non natural intelligences to broaden the scope and findings of this research.

III. Theoretical framework of AI Philosophy: The sources of legitimacy to analyze artificial intelligence

The following work tries to unveil a complex reality, 1) where there are new rules attached to command and control and 2) to bring to light new ways of thinking. A framework for analysis, the Gil dashboard for legitimacy is developed. The dashboard allows for comparisons of most similar and most different cases. The theoretical framework is in the intersection between values and AI development, and allows to unveil how AI is mediating problems related to coordination and control, what uncertainties about the future society and the polity different countries face against AI development, and what could we say about different cultural values.

We depart from the work on legitimacy from Max Weber -for whom there exist three types of domination, charismatic, traditional and rational or legal [6]. This framework was revised by Matheson [7] in 1987, nearly a century after Weber started writing. Matheson qualifies and opposes Max Weber theory on legitimacy. Later on, and departing from Matheson, this work develops a theoretical framework to allow for the comparison of AI legitimacy bases in the European Union, the United States and China - and could be valuable for the analysis of developing countries, and countries in the global south.

Weber distinction among the three types of domination differentiating three types of domination, charismatic, traditional and rational or legal is based on the legitimacy of the power-holder. The work by Matheson nearly a century later includes eight types of domination, including the perspective of both the power holders and the power subjects. The main critique that Matheson introduces to Weber's work is that democracy and its effects along the XX century are not reflected in Max Weber typology. Matheson reaches new layers of granularity for the study of the polity and society with his revised proposal. From Matheson´s critique of Weber I develop the following table: The table explains visually the eighth types of domination. This would be an eight dimensional view of sources of legitimacy.

TABLE I. The eight dimensional view of sources of legitimacy, by Olga Gil

Dimension	Definition of the dimension
Convention	Norms, rules: legal or customary rules that prescribe forms of behavior
Contract as basis of legitimacy	Mutual rights and obligations. The theory of consent as the basis of obligations
Basis of legitimacy in a conformity with universal principles: natural law	Theories of natural law, aka, the existence of a natural order superior to man-made law
Sacredness of authority	Power-holder or his/her norms considered to be sacred divine right of reigns. For Max Weber it could also be an attribute of an office rather than a person
Legitimacion by expertise	Technical expertise, in the vein defended by Saint-Simon, Taylorian theories, or historic laws
A popular mandate in a constitutional democracy	Popular mandate: a claim to democratic election in accordance with constitutional procedures. Based on constitutionalism, power holders elected in accordance with constitutional procedures. Here we find a distinction between polulist democracies, where the will of a majority rules, and constitutional democracies, were there will of the majority is limited by a constitution
Personal relation	Domination in which there are close ties between power-holders and power-subjects such as personal authority or paternal authority relationships
Personal quality of the power holder	Domination based on the personal quality of the power holder, by virtue of which he/she can claim a right of command

Having AI in mind and looking at this framework for the analysis of the cases selected, observations about new sources of legitimacy out of the scope of the table above can be drawn. A first one would be coercion as an instrument for legitimacy. A second source of legitimacy would be AI development outside the umbrella of the state, based in ethics codes. For instance, an applied comparison of national AI strategies in nine countries, including China and the United States finds that national AI strategies have an approach towards AI governance that entails cooperation among the public sector, industry and academia and is based on ethics [8]. For this purpose cooperation is achieved with voluntary mechanisms including best practices, codes of conduct, and guidelines.

IV. Method as a source of change and legitimacy

A third source of legitimacy would be linked to method. Matheson's approach to sources of legitimacy reviews Max Weber work making important contributions. However, the search of improved democracies through method as a source of legitimacy -a type of legitimacy based in experimenting with method and in an active process, not only based in a popular mandate, to reach better results- is not included in Matheson analysis. Method is the base to reach new knowledge following the scientific revolution in Europe. Method, in contrast, has not been explored as a feature to improve democratic governments. The result is that there has not been an appraisal of method as a way to reach better results in democratic regimes. An example of the dangers and limitations of not including method as a source of improved legitimacy is the work comparing national AI strategies in nine countries, including China and the United States [8], stressing the lack of concrete mechanisms for inclusion of civic society and public engagement in AI control. Moreover, at the core of a general approach to use ethic guidelines as an efficient measure to prevent or reduce harm caused by AI the general argument is for its higher flexibility, as opposed to hard regulations that could represent an obstacle to economic and technical innovation [8] [9], or other means of legitimacy.

These new sources of legitimacy will be incorporated in the previous table in order to develop a new table, the Gil Dashboard, allowing us to analyze artificial intelligence from a comparative perspective. The sources of legitimacy are incorporated close to the category that is more akin to the concept, if any. Additions are included in bold text.

TABLE II. THE GIL DASHBOARD: THIRTEEN SOURCES OF LEGITIMACY TO ANALYZE AI

Dimension	Definition of the dimension
Convention	Norms, rules: legal or customary rules that prescribe forms of behavior
Contract as basis of legitimacy	Mutual rights and obligations. The theory of consent as the basis of obligations
Basis of legitimacy in a conformity with universal principles: natural law	Theories of natural law, aka, the existence of a natural order superior to man-made law
Sacredness of authority	Power-holder or his/her norms considered to be sacred divine right of reigns. For Max Weber it could also be an attribute of an office rather than a person
Legitimation by **human** expertise	Technical expertise, in the vein defended by Saint-Simon, Taylorian theories, or historic laws
Legitimation based on an algorithm	**Legitimation based on macrodata –hindering the idea of individual liberty**
A popular mandate in a constitutional democracy	Popular mandate: a claim to democratic election in accordance with constitutional procedures. Based on constitutionalism, power holders elected in accordance with constitutional procedures. Here we find a distinction between populist democracies, where the will of a majority rules, and constitutional democracies, were there will of the majority is limited by a constitution
Improved democracies through method	**A type of legitimacy based not only in a popular mandate but experimenting with method and in a continuous process in order to reach better results, including accountability**
Regimes -non democracies- developed through method	**A type of legitimacy based on experimenting with method and a continuous process to justify objectives and reached results**
Personal relation	Domination in which there are close ties between power-holders and power-subjects such as personal authority or paternal authority relationships
Personal quality of the power holder	Domination based on the personal quality of the power holder, by virtue of which he/she can claim a right of command
Coercion	**The use of power to influence someone to do something they do not want to do, from exerting fear to nudging as positive reinforcement**
Societal cooperation, excluding the polity	**Development of mechanisms of cooperation among the public sector, industry and academia: cooperation is achieved with voluntary mechanisms including best practices, ethical codes of conduct, and guidelines**

V. CONCLUSIONS

This work allows us to unveil a complex reality from the perspective of philosophy, political theory and sociology, where AI brings new rules attached to command and control to governance in general. The Gil dashboard proposed shows how AI is mediating problems related to coordination and control in governance. This theoretical dashboard could be also useful to apply in a comparative perspective, in countries in Asia, western countries and countries in the global south. The dashboard brings to light new ways of thinking in methodological terms [10]. It also allows to address and reflect upon the following changes of present societies:

a) What uncertainties about the future society and the polity countries face against AI development?

b) What can it be said about cultural values?

c) What may we find in the intersection between values and AI development?

ACKNOWLEDGMENTS

The author wants to acknowledge the comments of five anonymous reviewers, which helped to improve the final manuscript when the paper was accepted for presentation at IARIA Annual Congress on Frontiers in Science, Technology, Services, and Applications, Venice, Italy April 24 - 28. The author also wants to acknowledge the inspiration of Prof. Joaquín Abellán, teaching together at the Master on Political Theory and Democratic Culture at UCM in the 2000-2022 editions, and to Prof. Carmelo Moreno´s comments at the 2022 AECPA Congress in Girona (Spain).

REFERENCES

[1] World Bank Group. Harnessing artificial intelligence for development in the post-covid-19 era. A Review of National AI Strategies and Policies. May 2021.

[2] Eichler, William. "'Shockingly small' number of councils embrace automation". LocalGov. 10 May 2019. https://www.localgov.co.uk/Shockingly-small-number-of-councils-embrace-automation-study-reveals/47387, retrieved october 20th, 2022.

[3] Justo-Hanani, Ronit. The politics of Artificial Intelligence regulation and governance reform in the European Union. Policy Sciences, 2022, vol. 55, no 1, p. 137-159.

[4] Ding, Jeffrey. Promoting nationally, acting locally: China´s next generation AI approach. In NESTA. The AI Powered State. China´s Approach to public innovation. 2020. P. 11-17.

[5] Ding, Jeffrey. Deciphering China's AI Dream: The Context, Components, Capabilities, and Consequences of China's Strategy to Lead the World in AI. Future of Humanity Institute, Oxford University. 2018.

[6] Abellán, Joaquín. El político y el científico: Weber. Madrid, Alianza Editorial. 2021.

[7] Matheson, Craig. Weber and the Classification of Forms of Legitimacy. British Journal of Sociology, 1987, p. 199-215.

[8] Gianni, Robert; Lehtinen, Santtu; Nieminen, Mika. Governance of responsible ai: from ethical guidelines to cooperative policies. Frontiers in Computer Science, 2022, vol. 4.

[9] Gianni, Letizia. Democratic Accountability in Stressful Times: When Decisions Must Be Made Quickly. Penn State Journal of Law & International Affairs, 2023, vol. 11, no 1, p. 1.

[10] Moreno, Carmelo. "Los fundamentos de la política. La noción de política, las teorías sobre el concepto de poder y el dilema de legalidad vs. legitimidad política." Análisis de la política. Enfoques y herramientas de la Ciencia Política, Mikel Barreda. 2016.

Design of Personalized Recommender System based on Hybrid Filtering and Fog Computing Architecture

Survey of Recent Personalized Recommender Systems in Ubiquitous and IoT environment

Noura Abdaoui
National School of Computer Sciences (ENSI)
University of Manouba, Tunisia
E-mail: noura.abdaoui@gmail.com

Ismahene Hadj Khalifa, Sami Faiz
Higher Institute of Multimedia Arts of Manouba (ISAMM)
University of Manouba, Tunisia
E-mail: ismaheneawatef.hadjkhalifa@isamm.uma.tn, sami.faiz@isamm.uma.tn

***Abstract*—Ubiquitous recommendation systems aim to provide users personalized recommendations of online products or services. Various recommendations techniques have been developed to fulfill the needs in different scenarios. This paper presents a survey of recent Personalized Recommender Systems in Ubiquitous and Internet of Things (IoT) environment, followed by an in-depth analysis of groundbreaking advances in recommendation systems based on big data. Furthermore, this paper discusses the issues faced in modern recommendation systems, such as sparsity, scalability, and diversity and illustrates how these challenges can be transformed into personalized recommender model that is described in the final Section. The novel recommender model aims to integrate hybrid filtering technique and fog architecture in order to generate contextual and personalized recommendations. The Fog computing architecture aims to solve the ubiquitous recommendations issues related to IoT challenges. As result, the given model is a multi-layer fog structure which is implemented in Smart shopping and used multi sources big data in order to propose personalized offers according to the users' profiles and analyze their feedbacks to improve their experiences.**

Keywords-Ubiquitous Recommender System; personalized recommendation; hybrid recommender approach; fog architecture; IoT.

I. INTRODUCTION

Ubiquitous recommender systems assist the mobile user by providing him with personalized recommendations of items or services that are in his device while context is the most important aspect [3] context-awareness as defined by [4] includes parameters, such as Location, Time, Date and Weather. Thereby in order to provide accurate recommendations, we have to let the system use the context and at the same time have our privacy respected. Nowadays, technologies have become ubiquitous and users tend to use smart devices to use the internet. These devices used connected sensors coming under IoT [5]. This is a new paradigm-shift from traditional interactions between mobile user and devices, which provides the ubiquitous computing environment.

This new paradigm paves the path for huge applications on the mobile user level to improve the quality of being or service, and on the decision-makers' level to afford an enduring raise in revenue. This has created enormous potential for ubiquitous recommender systems in many industries and domains to provide tailored recommendations for mobile users. Since, thus enhancing the patient's quality in smart health, the customer's shopping experience in smart marketing as well as the enterprise goal, and improving the smart traveling plans, etc. As we know, most of the IoT applications are connected with cloud computing. And this cloud gives the services as on-demand and scalable storage, along with processing facilities according to IoT application needs. According to [1] for real-time applications, 30 million clients are transferring data up to 25 000 records every second, which is not efficient for the cloud. Together with the growth of data quantity and the emergence of different kinds of dynamic end-user and access smart IoT devices, the information overload problem is becoming serious. To address these limitations, fog computing technology was first introduced by Cisco in 2012, which integrated edge devices and cloud resources [2].

The main objective of this paper is to describe and discuss the existing recommend approaches in different fields. Then, we will give a brief description of our novel recommender system that aims to integrate hybrid filtering approach and fog architecture in order to generate personalized and ubiquitous recommendation collected from dynamic and heterogeneous big data. The paper is structured as follows: Section II gives an introductory of the studies of ubiquitous computing , the recent state of the art recommendation systems in ubiquitous and Cloud computing with similar discussion of given issues. Subsequently, the integration of fog architecture in the proposed recommender system will be presented in Section III. Section IV describes the system's implementation and highlights the results. In Section V, we wrap up the paper with conclusions and horizons of work that would improve the suggested ubiquitous fog-based recommender system.

II. RELATED WORK

In this Section, we present the background and studies of ubiquitous computing. Then, different ubiquitous and fog recommender systems are shown in many sectors using different filtering techniques that exist in literature. Finally, we will discuss the different limitations to improve our novel recommender model in the future work.

A. *Ubiquitous Computing*

The term ubiquitous computing, was conceived by Mark Weiser in 1988 at Xerox PARC. It is an embedded computational technology in the form of a microprocessor in every object [3]. Ubiquitous computing can occur with any device, any time, any place and in any data format across the network technologies, such as RFID, Wi-Fi and Bluetooth. Moreover, in order for ubiquitous to be achieved, common objects that humans use daily are appeared and afford computational services without expecting from users to explicitly interact with them. Apart of ubiquitous research deals with Location-Based Information Systems. Such systems utilize the user's location as context to provide users with the ability to produce and access information that is related to a location. Thus, context is an information that can be used to characterize the situation of a user in his interaction. Consequently, Ubiquitous recommender systems facilitate users on location by providing them with personalized recommendations of items in the proximity via mobile devices.

A number of ubiquitous recommender systems (RS) challenges exist, ranging from technological, such as wireless technology limitations and storage limitations, to challenges related to context-awareness, tracking user intentions and privacy concerns [6]. Without forgetting the amount of information, a user has to access is often lost and left with a feeling of disappointment and frustration.

In the next subsections, we will present the several approaches used to make the RS.

B. *Collaborative Recommender System*

The Collaborative Filtering (CF) technique recommends items based on the similarity measures between users and items [7]. The system recommends those items that are preferred by similar category of users. The CF approach has been used for recommendations in the IoT. There are two main CF techniques: memory-based CF and model-based CF. In memory-based CF, user recommendations or predictions of ratings on future items are based on the users' rating behavior by using correlations between items or between users. Model-based CF is more scalable in cases where only the training set is used to make the pattern. It uses this pattern to recommend future ratings. Compared with memory-based CF, model-based CF is considered less accurate because of the large fraction among the item-user values in the training part of the dense dataset [10]. In [11], the authors proposed a unified CF model based on a probabilistic matrix factorization recommender system that exploits three kinds of relations in order to extract the latent factors among these relations: user–user, thing–user and thing–thing. The author in [12] exploited the CF method to design an IoT trust and reputation model that investigated trust and reputation among IoT nodes and Probabilistic Neural Networks (PNN). The Quality of Recommendation (QR) is defined as a score of trustworthiness. In [13], the CF approach was adapted to the weather and location data that were collected by the sensors to provide effective recommendations for the residents of that geographical region. It is the weather and location-aware recommendation system. A Ubiquitous Context Aware Recommender Systems for Ubiquitous Learning (UbiCARsUL) is proposed by [14]. The system enables students to scan QR Code tag attached to the corresponding plant in order to display related multimedia materials on the screen of mobile phones. This new paradigm uses Collaborative Filtering Approach in recommender systems, Clustering Algorithm for grouping students and Association Rules Algorithm in Data Mining for discovering interesting relations between variables. Smart devices are far connected in IoT to allow ubiquitous service access. This can produce heavy service redundant. Therefore, a recommender searching mechanism for trust-aware recommender system (TARS) is proposed to enhance CF in IoT environment by [17], named S_Searching: based on the scale-freeness of trust networks, selecting the global highest-degree nodes to construct a Skeleton, and looking for the recommenders via this Skeleton. Benefiting from the higher outdegrees of the nodes in the Skeleton, S_Searching can find the recommenders efficiently. S_Searching can find almost the same number of recommenders as that of conducting full search, which is much more than that of applying the classical searching system in the scale-free network, while the computational complexity and cost is much less. But, the research on the recommender searching mechanism of TARS is still always at the beginning stage. It is not easy to find the most reliable recommenders for the active users in the scale-free network.

However, Collaborative Filtering (CF) suffers from many problems, such as :

- Scalability RSIoT deals with a large amount of data that need computation power to conduct the recommendations, as well as fast response to online user requirements.
- Cold start problem particularly when a new user joins the system.
- Data sparsity may affect the accuracy of collaborative RS.

C. *Contetnt-Based Recommender System*

In Content-Based Filtering CBF [23] methods, the algorithm recommends items or similar to those items that were liked in past. It examines previously rated items and recommends best matching item. The CBF approach also has been used for recommendations in the IoT. SOMAR is a recommender system proposed by [20], which aims to suggest activities to user and the data used are based on Facebook and sensor data. In [21], the authors adapted CBF approach in medicine to recommend a suitable activity plan for the patient's data through their medical sensors that can be worn and a virtual nurse explains this. In [22], the authors adapted a CBF approach to building a recommendation module for their smart restaurant, which aims to provide dish recommendations based on the customers' tracking history.

A natural limitation of Content-Based Filtering is the need to have a generic and rich representation of the content of the items. Moreover, this type of system generally suffers from the problem of overspecialization; for example, when a user likes an event (e.g. ads of discount pricing) during shopping, it does not mean that he will want to see it again. However, using a CBF approach, the system will suggest him to come-back a second time to the same place with the same type of event (even if it is not organized). When he might be more interested in events, he did not discover on the last shopping.

D. Knowledge-based Recommender System

Knowledge-based approach suggests products based on inferences about user's needs and preferences. It is based on the identified relationship between a user's need and a possible recommendation [24]. Ontology is a formal method of representing knowledge that is central to building RSIoT. For example, the authors in [25] proposed a method for generating automatic rules and recommending the best rule. The user has the opportunity to add new rules for newly connected devices. Three ontology models were created: (i) Things, which provides all information for things; (ii) Context, which provides contextual information about people, environment and things and (iii) Functionality, which links the functionality of context and things. For smart health applications, ontology plays a significant role in building a recommender system. [26] Adapted a fuzzy ontology to build a system that monitors diabetes patients and recommends specific food and drugs.

However, such models still face major issues, which cannot treat decisions that have no rules allied to the system, and needs knowledge engineering in the building, and can be expensive.

E. Hybrid Recommender System

Hybrid recommender approach [27] is the one that combines multiple recommendation techniques together to produce the output with higher accuracy. A lot of research work has been done to peruse the healthy life style, by employing machine learning algorithms on past user activity data, heart rate data, and accelerometer data to identify the type of activity, and/or estimate caloric consumption. PROFIT [28] is a hybrid recommendation system that matches the user's profile to available activities according to his geo-location and time availability. It is a personalized fitness assistant framework that integrates activity data collected by the user's smart phone, their preferences and fitness goals, their availability and their social network. Then, it automatically generates fitness schedules and socially enhanced recommendations of new activities, as well as fitness buddies by using the collaborative filtering. FOBA [5] is a fog computing system aims to recommend products of a banking entity. The solution developed by a hybrid method of recommendation: Collaborative Filtering combined with Content-Based Filtering.

F. Recommendations with machine learning (ML)

ML algorithms can be divided into three (supervised, unsupervised and semi supervised), based on the nature of the data involved. Many studies of RS have investigated this approach. In [16], the authors designed the Optimal State-based Recommender System by exploiting ML algorithms as Distributed Kalman Filters, Distributed mini-batch SGD and Distributed Alternating Least Square based classifier and some ML platforms. In [18], a recommendation engine that provides personalized wearable technologies recommendations for proactive monitoring. The framework consists of three main models: (i) the classifier model; (ii) the optimization model, (iii) the Monitoring Framework. Rasch in [19] adapted unsupervised learning to build an RS for smart homes. The system learns user patterns and conducts recommendations based on user contexts. A decision tree [8] is used to build a system that provides lifecare recommendations. A personalized recommendation system for e-commerce based on big data analysis is improved by [9]. The system is divided into four levels, which are data layer, management layer, business layer and presentation layer, and each layer is closely related to big data. The results improve that the text matching algorithm used in the system can define the membership of goods with the search keywords input by customers. But When the method is applied to full goods search, due to the variety of goods, the proposed method is difficult to understand when selecting the representative features and defining membership, so it needs further study. With the increase of IoT connected devices, the amount of data has increased. Many research contributions have employed ontology-based semantic approaches to improve the access and integration of heterogeneous information from various sources in many areas. ProTrip, a health-centric tourism recommender system has been proposed by [29]. It based on hybrid filtering, which is capable of suggesting the food availability through considering climate attributes based on user's personal choice and nutritive value.

G. Discussion of recommender system's challenges

Nevertheless, despite the success of ubiquitous recommender systems in IoT research there is still room for more studies to resolve many constraints as:

- Scalability. Traditional algorithms will face scalability issues as the number of users and items increases. However, recommendation systems must respond to the user's needs immediately, regardless of the user's rating history and purchase situation, which requires high scalability [30].
- Sparsity. Many commercial recommendation systems use big data, and the user-item matrix used for filtering may be very large and sparse. Therefore, the performance of the recommendation process may be degraded due to the cold start problems caused by data sparsity [31].
- Diversity. Unfortunately, some traditional algorithms may accidentally do the opposite because they always recommend popular and highly-rated items that some specific users love. Therefore, new hybrid methods need to be developed to improve the performance of the recommendation systems [32].

III. INTEGRATION OF FOG COMPUTING ARCHITECTURE FOR IMPLEMENTING THE PROPOSED RECOMMENDER SYSTEM

Fog computing expands the traditional cloud by adding an intermediate layer between mobile users and the cloud, where the new layer involves fog servers directly used near mobile users and IoT devices. The integration of fog architecture in the proposed recommender system with the influx of huge amounts of data referred to big data is a crucial axis of the proposed model. This solution aims to provide intelligent tools to target and recommend the personalized offers according to the mobile users' profile, and to track and analyze their feedbacks to improve the customers experiences and predict their demands. The proposed architecture consists of three main layers as presented in Figure 1, which are IoT layer , Fog layer and cloud layer.

- Things Layer: is the layer closest to the end mobile user and ubiquitous environment where data is generated. This layer contains the mobile user sensors that operate to feed the system with data.
- Fog Layer: contains a number of decentralized fog nodes in each given location. Fog nodes have the potential to reduce the amount of data transmitted to the cloud layer and minimize the request response time for ubiquitous recommendations. Moreover, the fog nodes are also connected with cloud data center by IP core network.
- Cloud data center Layer: is the top layer of the architecture consists of multiple high-performance servers, storage devices and network access to shared resources over the IoT network. Thus, Cloud performs the "heavy services" of data analysis and processing that fog cannot perform, such as big data processing.

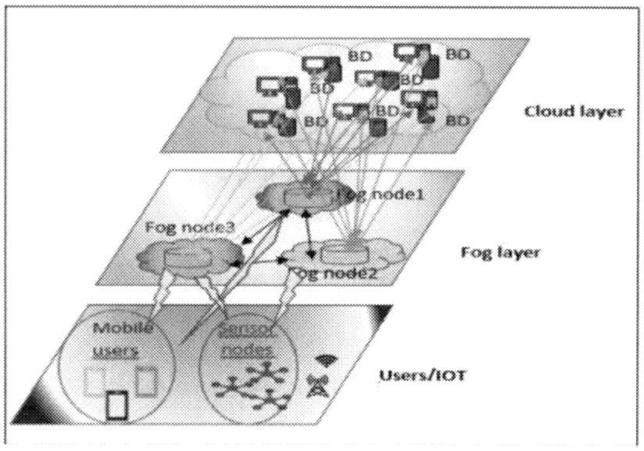

Figure 1. Fog architecture for implementing the recommender system

The principle of the designed model is that each mobile user should be connected with different fog nodes (fog server) in different floors by wireless access technologies Wi-Fi. Each fog server is linked into the cloud by IP core network. This architecture provides efficient data processing and storage services because each fog node represents RS that has a number of mobile users interfaces connected to both layers: IoT 's sensors, mobile users, other intelligent devices and the cloud layer. The RS provides personalized and contextual preferences recommendations to mobile user. Many resident modules are parts of the Context-A ware RS, including big data resources, new users, recommendations, list of personalized offers. Therefore, hybrid algorithm is implemented combined Content-Based Filtering and Collaborative Filtering to build the recommendations list. The goal is to rank most suitable content from contextual preference and user's profile. Then according required information and his interaction with fog nodes, we provide personalized recommendations.

As Figure 2 shows, there are four principal components in the proposed Personalized Recommender System Architecture namely; mobile user profile, Process of ubiquitous fog recommendations, mobile user interface and the fog data processing.

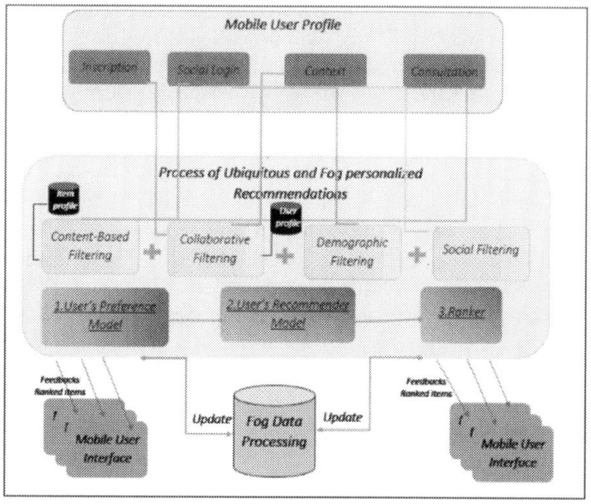

Figure 2. Personalized RS Architecture

A. *Mobile User Profile*

The user's profile can be extracted from many sources. Like inscription or by social login, even without log-in: such as frequency and duration of browsing, number of clicks, scrolling, etc. Also, through integrating contextual information (location, time, physical environment, ...). The data collected about the mobile user are then selected, analyzed, and saved as independent modules. These modules are combined to build the "user profile". A profile will contain information that can be used to determine mobile user's preferences in terms of items.

B. *Process of ubiquitous and fog personalized recommendations*

The process takes as input all the modules that constitute the target user's profile:

- The Content-Based Filtering describes the characteristics of center activities that the mobile user has consulted in the past in the form of key-word vectors. These key words are generally extracted automatically during the consultation or manually assigned during the inscription.
- The Collaborative Filtering contains the rating data of the consulted items and the user's context.
- Demographic filtering contains the user's demographic attributes. These attributes can either be entered by the user himself by filling in the registration form or extracted from his social login.

Once the mobile user profile modules are detected, recommendation approaches and the appropriate hybridization technique are selected, this process returns a list of items with the degrees of appreciation that the target user can give to each item. This process is detailed over several modules as shown below.

1) Update user's personal preference Model : it takes as input the historical data of a single user and outputs the user's contextual preference. Concerning the newly registered users for those the system has no historical data, a clustering block is designed using K-means [33] and Density-based spatial clustering of applications with noise (DBSCAN) [34] algorithms. These algorithms are used easily with any data type, various distance functions, and efficient indexing approaches facilitating the analysis of large datasets. According to the mobile user profiles of all the users, the system identifies clusters of users with similar profile information. Then, for each cluster, it collects the historical data of all the users belonging to that group. Next, the classification module used to learn a group-level contextual preference model. Having a clustering model and group-level contextual preference models for groups in hand, as soon as new user registers to the system. Finally, the group-level contextual preference model will be used as the user's personal preference model. The model will be in use until the system collects enough historical data from the new user for building a pure personal contextual preference model.

2) User's recommender Model : it receives as input the historical data of a single user or all users that belong to the cluster. To capture the user context, each historical data of user is made of the most recent user profile information, the offer (purchased or not). To create the training dataset, the system takes the received user data. Then, we use the data to find the best algorithm and best parameters and then save the final model. For each new offer, the system predicts the probability that the user will buy it and considers this value as the score of the offer; finally, offers are ranked according to their scores (i.e., the probability that they will be bought). To compute the prediction, and in particular to build the personal recommender models, we use popular classification algorithms is Bayes Search Cross-Validation (BSCV) [15], because it updates the current best model during each iteration and changes parameter settings according to the search ranges. Finally, we store the best model to be used in the future.

3) Ranker : for each personnalized offer, the system computes the offer's score (the probability of buyin the offer by user) using the user's recommender model. The Ranker receives the corresponding preference model of the user. Then, we obtain, for each offer, the probability that it will be bought by the user and use that as the offer score. Finally, the Ranker sorts the travel offers according to their scores and presents them to the user.

C. Mobile user interface

After the ranked list of offers is shown to the user in the mobile user interface, the users will typically buy an offer from the list shown to them and ignore the rest. The user's historical data are updated with the offers in the list (where each offer is tagged as purchased/not purchased). This interface consists of collecting the feedback of the purchasing decision after the ranked recommendation. This interface supports interactions between the mobile user and the Context-Aware personalized system of recommendation.

D. Fog Data processing

In this module, raw datasets are filtered converted and stored into various databases. The aim of data filtering is to extract useful information to the recommender system. We categorize six databases that describe a way of identifying the dataset: Item Profile, User profile, User-Item Preference, Fog Server List, Contextual Information, Recommendation Output.

- Item Profile: this database contains item attributes, such as item ID, description and category, and virtual content size.
- User's profile: this database contains user's attributes, such as age and gender.
- User-Item Preference: this database contains user-item preference information that has been converted from raw data. A preference could either be explicit or implicit.
- Fog Server List: fog server ID, workload capability, processing capability, storage capability and power usage.
- Contextual Information: this database contains contextual information such as user's localization, time, and network bandwidth information.
- Recommendation Output: this database contains the final output. It stores the output generated during the process of creating a recommendation, such as similarity matrix, training data and testing data.

The basic idea is to maximize the use of a fog server closer to the user. We try to process and store data as close as possible to the user who connects to the target fog server. If the target fog server cannot provide such a service, it will send a request to neighboring fog servers. If neighboring fog servers cannot provide the requested service, then the request will be sent to the cloud.

IV. IMPLEMENTATION OF THE PROPOSED RECOMMENDER SYSTEM

In the following Section, we implement the Ubiquitous fog recommender system in smart shopping by deploying five fog servers. We perform a set of experiment based on a real-world dataset.

A. Integration of Ubiquitous Fog-Based RS in Smart Shopping

Ubiquitous fog recommender system is evaluated using a dataset containing ID address, destination IP address, connected fog server IP address, and the localization of the mobile user. We treat each ID address as a user, because it is a unique identifier of his Mobile in our fog environment. An item could refer to Idsensor connected to a product or a web site visited by a person. In our use case, we have used many types of nodes in the three floors. Static nodes such as beacons attached to different products and fog nodes in the different floors. Also, we use mobile nodes such as mobile phone. Each mobile user is identified by his mobile's API. Mobile user sensor is detected by mobile devices which contact the fog node with the proximity information. We have deployed also the fog-based hybrid recommender system on each fog server and an Alibaba cloud server. The mobile user can access the Internet and use smart devices by connecting to the corresponding fog server. The dataset is obtained from the deployed fog servers.

We have used different platforms to simulate fog servers. A typical platform is Windows10 OS with Intel Core i5 CPU@2.7 GHz and 16 GB memory. All algorithms were implemented using python with the following installed libraries: NumPy, pandas, matplotlib, scikit-learn, nltk, scipy. Anaconda has been used for python package management and deployment. We collect 200 records of different users' interaction with different items in the mall. All data are obtained from the deployed five simulated fog servers. Due to the small amount of data set, we use all the data and split data into 80% for training purpose, 20% as test data set.

B. *Evaluation Data Utility vs RMSE and MAE*

In the following experiments, each floor which includes fog server is the target level. Any user connected to fog servers deployed on these floors is considered in location. In the experiments, we vary the weight value w_j and attempt identifying the best value of each parameter to obtain the most accurate result. We use two popular evaluation methods for recommendation, mean absolute error (MAE) and root-mean-square error (RMSE), to justify our quality of the prediction. RMSE, as in (1), penalizes large errors by amplifying the differences between the predicted preferences items and the real ones:

$$RMSE = \sqrt{\sum(test-rsl)^2/|test|}. \quad (1)$$

MAE, as in (2), is the average absolute deviation of the predicted ratings from the real ratings of items:

$$MAE = \sum|test-rsl|/test. \quad (2)$$

We set up a decay factor for the weight parameter wj to observe its impact on the prediction accuracy and data utility. Here, the decay factor has been set up as (w_j/n) for present location, the weight of the third level of location is $(w_j/n)^3$. wj is the weight at level j that controls prediction at each location level and affects the final prediction. The weights satisfy the following constraints: wj ε [0,1], w1+w2...+wj=1. In Figure 3, wj is fixed as 0.7, n varies from 1 to 4. This value has also been mapped to the amount of privacy levels, thus there are 4 privacy levels from ε [0, β] based on location.

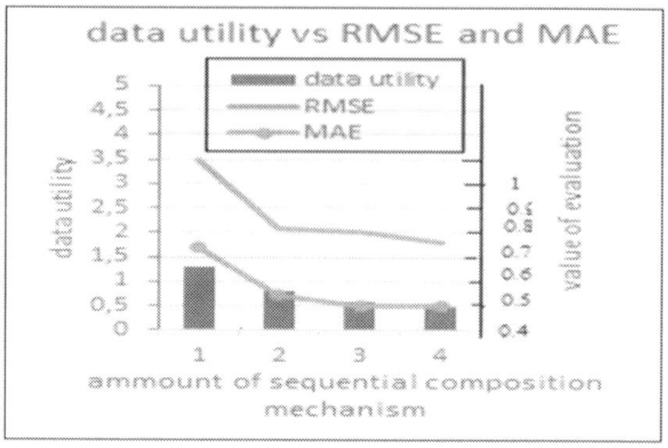

Figure 3. Data utility vs RMSE and MAE.

In Figure 3, we observe that all three measurements show a similar trend. The value of data utility decreases from 1.3 to 0. 5. The RMSE and MAE value both decreases. RMSE decreases from 3.5 to 0. 77. MAE decreases from 1.7 to 0. 5. If wj is higher, both MAE and RMSE results are better. If n is higher, both evaluation results are better as well. However, the trend becomes weaker.

C. *Evaluation Values of Precision and Recall*

Here, also each floor which includes fog server is the target level. w_k is the weight value of the target level. As a result, we need to be aware of the impact of recommended content size on the server. We use the recall and precision method to measure our result. Both methods (as defined in (3) and (4)) are broadly used in evaluating information retrieval and statistical classification. In general, precision represents the prediction accuracy, while recall represents the prediction scale. Ideally, both values would be high.

$$P = N\chi/N\rho. \quad (3)$$

$$R = N\chi/N\Phi. \quad (4)$$

$N\chi$ is the Number of correct items recommended and $N\rho$ is the Number of items recommended. $N\Phi$ is the Number of relevant and recommended items.

We vary the weight value w_k from 0 to 1 with the step size of 0,2 to observe the impact of result accuracy. We also modify the number of prediction items from 4 to 10 to observe the impact of result accuracy. In Figure 4, each band represents the change of the w_k from 0 to 1. The height of each point on a given band is the evaluation value of recall. The length between two points on a given band represents the difference between two results. Various bands represent different numbers of predictions, corresponding to items recommended to a fog server. A higher value of the prediction number means requiring more storage space on a fog server.

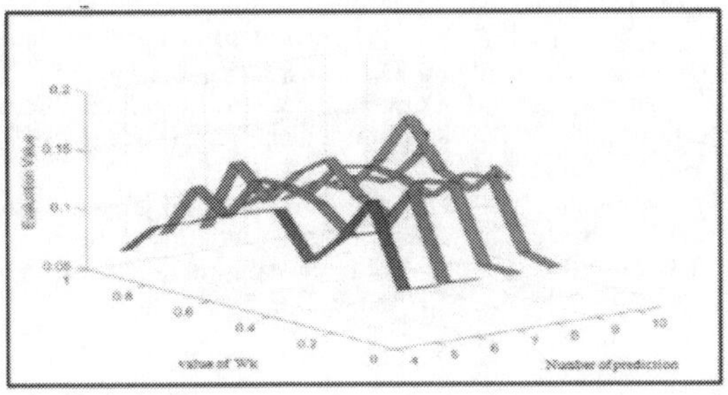

Figure 4. Evaluation value of recall.

Figure 4 shows that the more items are predicted, the higher the recall value is.

In Figure 5, the height of each point on a band represents the evaluation value of precision. We also observe that the more items are predicted, the lower the precision value. If w_k is 0.3, we obtain most accurate result on each band. So, if w_k is 0,3, we obtain the best evaluation results for both precision and recall. The prediction number does not impact the trend pattern of the evaluation value. However, the more items are predicted, the worse the predicted results are, and the higher the recall is.

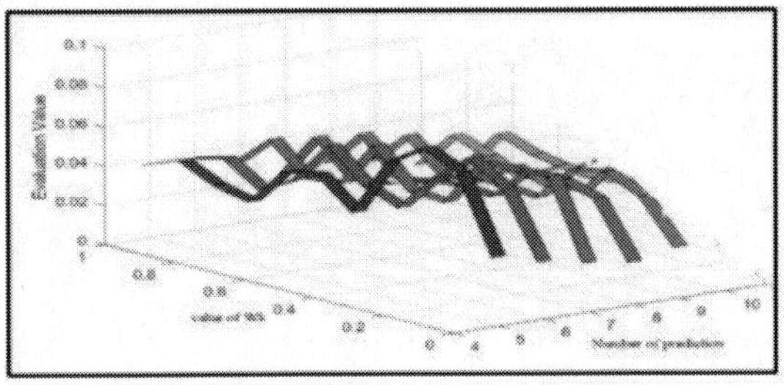

Figure 5. Evaluation value of precision.

The obtained results prove that the efficiency of Ubiquitous fog-based RS and its sample algorithms are feasible and can run independently from the cloud server. The system helps fog servers choose the most frequently requested content to purchase in order to save bandwidth, storage resources and used network resources. It also provides much more accurate recommendation results for certain items based on fog server location.

V. Conclusion and Future Work

In this research, we presented a literature review of the current recommender systems and then we discussed the different challenges in order to present our new conceptual framework of recommendation. The innovative aspect of designed model is how to address the problem of information overload ubiquitous environment, and become a tool of fog computing optimization. Further, the proposed system of recommendation improved the user's experience in the smart shopping center where we used IoT devices.

Experimental results demonstrated that Ubiquitous fog-based RS provided highly accurate and personalized recommendations to mobile users. It considered the fog server as well as contextual data of mobile user. Furthermore, it incorporated feedbacks collected from mobile users. Adding to that, it improved customers' experiences stored in the server and anticipated new users' needs. In future research, we intend to extend our proposal to areas with deep learning algorithms and reinforcement learning which can be used to improve the current research and overcome limitations.

References

[1] M . Mukherjee, R. Matam, L. Shu, L. Maglaras, M. A. Ferrag, N. Choudhury, and V. Kumar, "Security and privacy in fog computing: Challenges," IEEE Access, vol. 5, pp. 19293–19304, 2017.

[2] M. Chiang and T. Zhang, "Fog and iot: An overview of research opportunities," IEEE Internet of Things Journal, Vol. 3, No. 6, pp. 854–864, 2016.

[3] Christos Mettouris and George A. Papadopoulos, "Ubiquitous recommender systems," Computing, vol. 96, no. 3, pp. 223-257, 2014.

[4] G. Adomavicius, B. Mobasher, R. Francesco, and A. Tuzhilin, "Context-aware recommender systems," AI Magazine, vol. 32, no. 3, pp. 67-80, 2011.

[5] Elena Hernández-Nieves , Guillermo Hernández , Ana-Belén Gil-González , Sara Rodríguez-González , and Juan M. Corchado, "Fog computing architecture for personalized recommendation of banking products," Expert Systems With Applications, 2020.

[6] J. H. Hong, J. Ramos, and AK. Dey, "Toward personalized activity recognition systems with a semipopulation approach," IEEE Trans Human-Mach Syst, vol. 46, no. 1, pp. 101–112, 2016.

[7] Prateek Parhi, Ashish Pal, and Manuj Aggarwal, "A survey of methods of collaborative filtering techniques," 2017 International Conference on Inventive Systems and Control (ICISC), 2017.

[8] H. Yoo and K. Chung, "Mining-based lifecare recommendation using peer-to-peer dataset and adaptive decision feedback," Peer-to-Peer Networking and Applications, vol. 11, pp. 1309–1320, 2018.

[9] Hua Chen, "Personalized recommendation system of e-commerce based on big data analysis," Journal of Interdisciplinary Mathematics vol. 21, no. 5, pp. 1243-1247, 2018.

[10] X. Su and T. M. Khoshgoftaar, " A survey of collaborative filtering techniques," Advances in artificial intelligence, 2009.

[11] L. Yao, Q. Z. Sheng, A. H. Ngu, H. Ashman, and X. Li, "Exploring recommendations in internet of things," 37th international ACM SIGIR conference on Research & development in information retrieval, pp. 855–858, 2014.

[12] S. Asiri and A. Miri, "An iot trust and reputation model based on recommender systems," 14th Annual Conference on Privacy, Security and Trust (PST), pp. 561–568, 2016.

[13] S. Chakraverty and A. Mithal, "Iot based weather and location aware recommender system," 8th International Conference on Cloud Computing, Data Science & Engineering (Confluence), pp. 636–643, 2018.

[14] Sukanya Thiprak and Werasak Kurutach, "Ubiquitous computing technologies and Context Aware Recommender Systems for Ubiquitous Learning," 12th International Conference on Electrical Engineering/Electronics, Computer, Telecommunications and Information Technology (ECTI-CON), IEEE. 2015

[15] T. H. Chung, and J. W. Burdick, "Analysis of Search Decision Making Using Probabilistic Search Strategies," *IEEE Trans. Robot*, pp. 132–144, 2012.

[16] M. Sewak and S. Singh, "Iot and distributed machine learning powered optimal state recommender solution," Internet of Things and Applications (IOTA), International Conference on, pp. 101–106. IEEE, 2016.

[17] Weiwei Yuan , Donghai Guan, Lei Shu and Jianwei Niu, "Recommender Searching Mechanism for Trust Aware Recommender Systems in Internet of Things," Automatika, vol. 54, no. 4, pp. 427–437, 2013.

[18] S. Asthana, A. Megahed, and R. Strong, " A recommendation system for proactive health monitoring using iot and wearable technologies," AI & Mobile Services (AIMS), IEEE International Conference on, pp. 14–21. IEEE, 2017.

[19] K. Rasch, "An unsupervised recommender system for smart homes," Journal of Ambient Intelligence and Smart Environments, vol. 6, pp. 21–37, 2014.

[20] Zanda, Andrea, Santiago Eibe, and Ernestina Menasalvas, "SOMAR: A social mobile activity recommender," Expert Systems with Applications vol. 39, no. 9, pp. 8423-8429, 2017.

[21] S. P. Erdeniz, I. Maglogiannis, A. Menychtas, T. N. Trang Tran, and A. Felfernig "Recommender systems for iot enabled m-health applications," IFIP International conference on artificial intelligence applications and innovations, pp. 227–237, 2018.

[22] N. Koubai and F. Bouyakoub, "My restaurant: A smart restaurant with a recommendation system," International Journal of Computing and Digital Systems, vol. 8, pp. 143–156, 2019.

[23] Umair Javed, K. Shaukat, I. Hameed, Farhat Iqbal, Talha Mahboob Alam, and S. Luo, "A Review of Content-Based and Context-Based Recommendation Systems," Int. J. Emerg. Technol, 2021.

[24] Eva Zangerle and Christine Bauer, "Evaluating Recommender Systems: Survey and Framework," ACM Computing Surveys (CSUR), 2022.

[25] I. Hwang, M. Kim, and H. J. Ahn, "Data pipeline for generation and recommendation of the iot rules based on open text data," In Advanced Information Networking and Applications Workshops (WAINA), 30th International Conference on, pp. 238–242. IEEE, 2016.

[26] F. Ali, S. R. Islam, D. Kwak, P. Khan, N. Ullah, Sang-jo Yoo, and K.S. Kwak, "Type-2 fuzzy ontology–aided recommendation systems for iot–based healthcare," Computer Communications, vol. 119, pp. 138–155, 2018.

[27] Erion Çanon and Maurizio Morisio, "Hybrid recommender systems: A systematic literature review," Intelligent Data Analysis, vol. 21, no. 6, pp. 1487–1524, 2018.

[28] Saumil Dharia, Magdalini Eirinaki, Vijesh Jain, Jvalant Patel, Iraklis Varlamis, Jainikkumar Vora, and Rizen Yamauchi, "Social recommendations for personalized fitness assistance," Personal & Ubiquitous Computing, vol. 22, no. 2, pp. 245-257, 2018.

[29] V. Subramaniyaswamy, Gunasekarn Manogaran, R. Logesh, V. Vijayakumar, Naveen Chilamkurti, D. Malathi, and N. Senthilselvan, "An ontology-driven personalized food recommendation in IoT-based healthcare system," The Journal of Supercomputing, vol. 75, pp. 3184–3216, 2018.

[30] J. Shokeen and C. Rana, "A study on features of social recommender systems," Artificial Intelligence Review, vol. 53, no. 2, pp. 965–988, 2020.

[31] J. D. West, I. Wesley-Smith, and C. T. Bergstrom, "A recommendation system based on hierarchical clustering of an article-level citation network," IEEE Transactions on Big Data, vol. 2, no. 2, pp. 113–123, 2016.

[32] X. He and X. Ke, "Research summary of recommendation system based on knowledge graph," 3rd International Conference on Big Data Engineering, pp. 104–109, 2021.

[33] S. Lu, H. Yu, X. Wang, Q. Zhang, F. Li, Z. Liu, and F. Ning, "Clustering method of raw meal composition based on pca and kmeans," 37th Chinese Control Conference (CCC), pp. 9007–9010, 2018.

[34] A. Smiti and Z. Elouedi, "Dbscan-gm: An improved clustering method based on gaussian means and dbscan techniques," IEEE 16th International Conference on Intelligent Engineering Systems (INES)," pp. 573–578, 2012.

The Open Government Data Digital Disconnect: Observations on Open Data Support by Local Government in Ireland

Theo Lynn
Irish Institute of Digital Business
Dublin City University
Dublin, Ireland
Email: theo.lynn@dcu.ie

Jennifer Kennedy
Irish Institute of Digital Business
Dublin City University
Dublin, Ireland
Email: jennifer.kennedy@dcu.ie

Pierangelo Rosati
J.E. Cairnes School of Business & Economics
University of Galway
Galway, Ireland
Email: pierangelo.rosati@universityofgalway.ie

Grace Fox
Irish Institute of Digital Business
Dublin City University
Dublin, Ireland
Email: grace.fox@dcu.ie

Colm O'Gorman
DCU Business School
Dublin City University
Dublin, Ireland
Email: colm.ogorman@dcu.ie

Declan Curran
DCU Business School
Dublin City University
Dublin, Ireland
Email: declan.curran@dcu.ie

Kate Hynes
DCU Business School
Dublin City University
Dublin, Ireland
Email: kate.hynes@dcu.ie

***Abstract*—The 2019 European Union (EU) Open Data Directive requires that public sector data should be open by design and by default. The EU Digital Economy & Society Index ranked Ireland as second in terms of data maturity amongst the EU Member States. In Ireland, local government is administered by 31 local authorities. In light of the Open Data Directive being transposed into Irish law in 2021, this paper explores the commitment of local authorities in the Republic of Ireland to the provision of open data by examining their activity on data.gov.ie, the Irish national data portal, and the treatment of open data in local authority corporate plans and digital strategies. We find preliminary evidence of a disconnect between national policy and local government activities and a potential urban-rural divide with respect to local government open data provision.**

***Keywords*—open data; Public Sector Information; PSI, open government; open government data; e-government; local government; local authorities**

I. INTRODUCTION

Open data is defined as data that meets three conditions i.e., it is (i) accessible at no more than the cost of reproduction, without limitations based on user identity or intent, (ii) in a digital, machine readable format for interoperation with other data; and (iii) free of restriction on use or redistribution in its licensing conditions [1]. Open government data is concerned with making Public Sector Information (PSI) freely available.
in open formats and ways that enable public access and facilitate exploitation [2]. A wide range of political and social, economic, and operational and technical benefits have been ascribed to open data, and open government data specifically [3]. For example, the European Union (EU) [4] cite a number of reasons for supporting greater access to PSI and open data specifically including:

- stimulating economic growth and spur innovation: public data has significant potential for re-use in new products and services;
- helping address societal challenges with the development of innovative solutions such as in healthcare or in transport;
- enhancing evidence-based policymaking and increase efficiency in public administrations;
- becoming a critical asset for the development of new technologies, such as artificial intelligence (AI), which require the processing of vast amounts of high-quality data;
- fostering the participation of citizens in political and social life and increase the transparency of government.

in open formats and ways that enable public access and facilitate exploitation [2]. A wide range of political and social, economic, and operational and technical benefits have been ascribed to open data, and open government data specifically [3]. For example, the European Union (EU) [4] cite a number of reasons for supporting greater access to PSI and open data specifically including:

- stimulating economic growth and spur innovation: public data has significant potential for re-use in new products and services;
- helping address societal challenges with the development of innovative solutions such as in healthcare or in transport;
- enhancing evidence-based policymaking and increase efficiency in public administrations;
- becoming a critical asset for the development of new technologies, such as artificial intelligence (AI), which require the processing of vast amounts of high-quality data;
- fostering the participation of citizens in political and social life and increase the transparency of government.

The economic value of PSI should not be underestimated. A 2018 study by Deloitte suggests that the total direct economic value of PSI is expected to increase from a baseline of €52 billion in 2018 for the EU28 to €194 billion in 2030 [5].

Driven by these potential benefits, the European Union (EU) has sought to encourage, promote, and regulate the provision and (re)use of PSI for over a decade. More recently, the EU has shifted its emphasis from PSI to open government data. This support is reflected in the reframing by the EU of the 2003 Public Sector Information Directive as the 2019 Open Data Directive whose central principle is that public sector information data should be open by design and by default while ensuring a consistent level of protection of public interest objectives including the protection of personal data [6]. In effect, this means that public sector data in EU Member States should be considered open by default unless access is restricted or excluded [7]. It has been long-recognised that open data has little has little intrinsic value i.e., its value is created by its use [3]. A significant feature of the Open Data Directive is that the EU specifically recognises that not all data is equal.

Chapter V of the Directive specifically defines and prioritises high-value data sets. Article 14(2) defines high-value datasets as having the potential to (a) generate significant socioeconomic or environmental benefits and innovative ser-vices; (b) benefit a high number of users, in particular SMEs;
(c) assist in generating revenues; and (d) be combined with other datasets [6]. Article 13(1) refers to six initial thematic categories of high-value datasets - geospatial, earth observation and environment, meteorological, statistics, companies and company ownership, and mobility. [6]. Article 17 required Member States to transpose the Directive into local laws, regulations, and administrative provisions by 17 July 2021 [6].

The EU Digital Economy and Society Index (DESI) ranks EU Member States based on their commitment to open data based on an assessment of the Member State's open data policy, open data impact, open data portal, and open data quality [8]. In 2022, Ireland was ranked second of the EU28 countries for open data maturity with a score of 95% of the maximum available score. The 2019 Open Data Directive was transposed into Irish law by S.I. No. 376 of 2021, the European Communities (Open Data & Re-use of Public Sector Information) Regulations 2021 and came into force on 22 July 2021 [7]. As well as promoting and encouraging the sharing of open data by public sector bodies and emphasising the principle of open by design and default, Irish law requires that where data is made available for re-use in open format, this data must be linked to the national open data portal, data.gov.ie [7]. These regulations apply to all public sector bodies including local authorities [7]. Indeed, the Department of Public Expenditure and Reform Open Data Strategy 2017-2022 and the Office of the Government Chief Information Officer's (OGCIO) Public Service Data Strategy 2019 – 2023 strategies both reinforce the general principles of the Open Data Directive.

There are currently 31 local authorities in the Republic of Ireland - 26 county councils, three city councils (Cork, Dublin and Galway), and two city and county councils (Limerick and Waterford). This paper explores the commitment of local authorities in the Republic of Ireland to the provision of open data. The remainder of the paper is structured as follows; Section 2 outlines the data, methodology, results and discussion, and Section 3 concludes with the implications of the findings.

II. METHODS, RESULTS & DISCUSSION

The study involves all 31 local authorities in the Republic of Ireland. Data was collected in December and January 2023. Data on open data provision and public use was collected manually from data.gov.ie, the Irish national data portal. To assess the strategic commitment of a local authority to open data, corporate plans and digital strategies (where available) were reviewed for references to open data.

As of January 2023, data.gov.ie featured 14,812 datasets from 160 publishers. Our results suggest 20 (65%) of the 32 local authorities were registered as publishers on data.gov.ie although three of the registered local authorities had yet to publish a dataset. The 20 local authorities registered represent 12.5% of publishers on data.gov.ie. In total, the remaining 17 local authorities had published 1,152 datasets. Local authorities represent a mere 7.8% of all datasets on data.gov.ie. The average number of datasets published by the 17 active local authorities on data.gov.ie was 67. Only five of the 12 local authorities published more than the average. The 20 local authorities registered represent 12.5% of publishers on data.gov.ie. In total, the remaining 17 local authorities had published 1,152 datasets. Local authorities represent a mere 7.8% of all datasets on data.gov.ie. The average number of datasets published by the 17 active local authorities on data.gov.ie was 67. Only five of the 12 local authorities published more than the average. The local authority dataset average is significantly lower than the average for data.gov.ie as a whole, i.e., 93 datasets. Six local authorities account for over 84% (968) of the published datasets, four of which are associated with the greater Dublin area (Dublin City Council, Fingal County Council, South Dublin County Council, and Dun Laoghaire-Rathdown County Council) and a further two in Connacht located in the West of the country i.e., Roscommon County Council and Galway County Council. Six city councils and county councils located fully in the functional urban area of cities accounted for 56% (646) of all datasets suggesting a significant urban-rural divide with respect to open dataset availability. Of the remaining 506 datasets, one county council, Roscommon, accounts for 56% (284) of the datasets.

TABLE I
DATA.GOV.IE PUBLISHER STATUS, DATASETS AND VIEWS BY LOCAL AUTHORITY.

Local Authority	Registered Publisher	Datasets (No.)	Datasets (%)	Views (No.)	Views (%)
Carlow CC	No	0	0%	0	0%
Cavan CC	No	0	0%	0	0%
Clare CC	Yes	5	0%	212	0%
Cork CiC	Yes	26	2%	8407	4%
Cork CC	No	0	0%	0	0%
Donegal CC	Yes	1	0%	1533	1%
Dublin CiC	Yes	110	10%	137404	72%
Dun Laoghaire-Rathdown CC	Yes	61	5%	8075	4%
Fingal CC	Yes	271	24%	5637	3%
Galway CiC	Yes	27	2%	29	0%
Galway CC	Yes	91	8%	1242	1%
Kerry CC	No	0	0%	0	0%
Kildare CC	Yes	14	1%	4216	2%
Kilkenny CC	Yes	18	2%	476	0%
Laois CC	No	0	0%	0	0%
Leitrim CC	No	0	0%	0	0%
Limerick CCC	Yes	0	0%	0	0%
Longford CC	No	0	0%	0	0%
Louth CC	Yes	0	0%	0	0%
Mayo CC	Yes	2	0%	1547	1%
Meath CC	No	0	0%	0	0%
Monaghan CC	No	0	0%	0	0%
Offaly CC	Yes	0	0%	0	0%
Roscommon CC	Yes	284	25%	1147	1%
Sligo CC	Yes	8	1%	360	0%
South Dublin CC	Yes	151	13%	7037	4%
Tipperary CC	No	0	0%	0	0%
Waterford CCC	No	0	0%	0	0%
Westmeath CC	Yes	11	1%	61	0%
Wexford CC	Yes	22	2%	2455	1%
Wicklow CC	Yes	47	4%	9821	5%

Notes: CC: County Council; CiC: City Council; CCC: City and County Council.

TABLE II
SUBSTANTIVE REFERENCES TO OPEN DATA IN CORPORATE PLANS OR DIGITAL STRATEGIES BY LOCAL AUTHORITY.

Local Authority	Corporate Plan	Digital Strategy
Carlow CC	N	NA
Cavan CC	N	N
Clare CC	N	N
Cork CiC	Y	Y
Cork CC	N	N
Donegal CC	N	NA
Dublin CiC	N	NA
Dun Laoghaire-Rathdown CC	N	Y
Fingal CC	N	Y
Galway CiC	N	NA
Galway CC	N	Y
Kerry CC	N	N
Kildare CC	N	NA
Kilkenny CC	N	NA
Laois CC	N	N
Leitrim CC	N	NA
Limerick CCC	N	Y
Longford CC	N	Y
Louth CC	N	NA
Mayo CC	N	NA
Meath CC	N	N
Monaghan CC	Y	N
Offaly CC	N	N
Roscommon CC	N	NA
Sligo CC	N	Y
South Dublin CC	N	Y
Tipperary CC	N	Y
Waterford CCC	N	Y
Westmeath CC	N	Y
Wexford CC	N	NA
Wicklow CC	N	Y

Notes: CC: County Council; CiC: City Council; CCC: City & County Council.

Dataset views was used as a proxy for utility. The 1,152 datasets published by Irish local authorities generated 189,659 views, an average of 6,118 views per dataset. Dublin City Council alone accounts for 72% of all local authority dataset views and the greater Dublin functional area accounts for over 83% of all local authority dataset views. The urban-rural divide is further emphasised when views from other cities are included rising to nearly 88% of views. Table I summarises our findings by website. In a recent study of 146 cities worldwide by the United Nations Local Online Services Index (LOSI) found that 46% of the city portals assessed for the LOSI 2022 study provide open data [11]. Against this backdrop, 17 active open data publishers representing 54% of local authorities may be viewed in a positive light. However, LOSI measure cities from a wide range of countries worldwide, most of which are outside of the EU where open data provision is regulated

To evaluate the strategic commitment and prioritisation of open data for local authorities in the sample, the most recent corporate plan and the most recent digital strategy (where available) were reviewed for references to open data.

Table II summarises our findings by website. First, while nearly all local authority corporate plans reference a desire to be open and transparent and a significant number listing the national open data plan in their reports, only two local authorities include a substantive reference in their corporate plan. Second, as can be seen from Table II, eleven local authorities did not have a current digital strategy accessible on their website. Of the remaining 20 local authorities, 12 had a substantive reference to open data in their digital strategy. However, despite the widespread lack of documented strategy, this should not be interpreted as a lack of open data prioritisation. Both Dublin City Council and Roscommon County Council, for example, have significant presences on data.gov.ie (see Table I), and both have their own data portal, and its own data portal, data.smartdublin.ie. and data - roscoco.opendata.arcgis.com.

III. CONCLUSIONS

Our results suggest that there is a disconnect between the EU and national policies and plans for open data and local authorities. This surfaces both in a lack of strategic intent as evidenced by the dearth of references to open data in local authority corporate plans, by a lack of action as evidenced by the relatively small number of datasets being contributed by local authorities, and finally by a lack of impact as evidenced by the number of views per dataset. Extant research posits a wide range of implementation and barriers to use that impede open government data projects including an inability to extract value from the data, local government willingness to share data, task complexity and individual or institutional skills and capabilities, amongst others [3] [12] [13]. In sum, there are challenges in will and skill for both data providers and users that need to be understood and overcome if the much-vaunted benefits of open data are to be accrued.

Our results also suggest a potential urban rural divide with respect to the provision and re-use of open data. In our sample, the greater Dublin area accounts for 83% of the open data provided by local authorities on data.gov.ie. Even if high-value datasets that generate significant socioeconomic or societal value are provided and exploited, they are likely to be biased towards urban communities thereby exacerbating existing digital and societal divides.

In many respects while the Open Data Directive and associated regulations require local authorities to make PSI available by default and design, enforcement, and indeed exploitation, is effectively left to the public. Janssen et al. [3] note that merely publishing and providing open government data is not enough, open data is only value when used, not only citizens and companies but the public sector. Ten years ago, Bertot et al. [13] noted a lack of evaluative metrics for open government data. Today, international benchmarks such as DESI and LOSI, and to some extent this paper, are limited due to their continued emphasis on supporting policies, availability of open government data and input-related metrics, such as the number of datasets, views, and downloads, rather than outcomes from the use of open data. To paraphrase Golding [14], open government data has "the potential to nourish and enhance the public sphere" but not without fixing the disconnect between national and local government policy and action, and the provision and exploitation of open data.

ACKNOWLEDGEMENTS

This research was partially funded by the Irish Department of Rural and Community Development with additional support from .IE, the official registry of .ie domain names.

REFERENCES

[1] HM Government. Open data white paper – "Unleashing the potential". 2012. [retrieved: month, year]

[2] E. Kalampokis, E. Tambouris, and K. Tarabanis, "A classification scheme for open government data: towards linking decentralised data", International Journal of Web Engineering and Technology, Jan 1, vol. 6, no. 3, pp. 266-85, 2011.

[3] M. Janssen, Y. Charalabidis, and A. Zuiderwijk, "Benefits, adoption barriers and myths of open data and open government", Information systems management, Sep 1, vol. 29, no.4, pp.258-68, 2012.

[4] European Commission, "Open Data". Available online: https://ec.europa.eu/digital-single-market/en/open-data.

[5] Deloitte, "Study to support the review of Directive 2003/98/EC on the re-use of public sector information". 2018.

[6] European Union, "Directive (EU) 2019/1024 of the European Parliament and of the Council of 20 June 2019 on open data and the re-use of public sector information", Official Journal of the European Union, 26 June 2019.

[7] C. Menton, "Circular 20/2021 - Open Data Directive", Department of Public Expenditure and Reform, DPE 212/007/2020, 2021.

[8] European Commission, "Digital Economy and Society Index (DESI) 2022", Digital public services, 2022.

[9] Open Government Unit, "Open Data Strategy 2017 – 2022", Department of Public Expenditure and Reform, 2017.

[10] Office of the Government Chief Information Officer, "Public Service Data Strategy 2019-2023", Department of Public Expenditure and Reform, 2021.

[11] United Nations, "United Nations e-government survey 2022", UN, 2022.

[12] J. A. Bichard and G. Knight, "Improving public services through open data: public toilets", Proceedings of the Institution of Civil Engineers-Municipal Engineer, Sep, vol. 165, no. 3, pp. 157-165, Thomas Telford Ltd, 2012.

[13] C. Martin, "Barriers to the open government data agenda: Taking a multi-level perspective", Policy Internet, Sep, vol. 6, no. 3, pp. 217-40, 2014.

[14] J. C. Bertot, P. McDermott, and T. Smith, "Measurement of open government: Metrics and process" 45th Hawaii International Conference on System Sciences, IEEE, Jan 4, pp. 2491-2499, 2012

[15] P. Golding, "World wide wedge: division and contradiction in the global information infrastructure" Monthly review, Jul 1, vol. 48, no. 3, pp. 70, 1996.

Web Accessibility of Irish Local Government Websites

Theo Lynn
Irish Institute of Digital Business
Dublin City University
Dublin, Ireland
e-mail: theo.lynn@dcu.ie

Jennifer Kennedy
Irish Institute of Digital Business
Dublin City University
Dublin, Ireland
e-mail: jennifer.kennedy@dcu.ie

Pierangelo Rosati
J.E. Cairnes School of Business & Economics
University of Galway
Galway, Ireland
e-mail: pierangelo.rosati@universityofgalway.ie

Grace Fox
Irish Institute of Digital Business
Dublin City University
Dublin, Ireland
e-mail: grace.fox@dcu.ie

Colm O'Gorman
DCU Business School
Dublin City University
Dublin, Ireland
e-mail:
colm.ogorman@dcu.ie

Declan Curran
DCU Business School
Dublin City University
Dublin, Ireland
e-mail:
declan.curran@dcu.ie

Kate Hynes
DCU Business School
Dublin City University
Dublin, Ireland
e-mail : kate.hynes@dcu.ie

***Abstract*—The European Union Web Accessibility Directive requires public sector bodies in EU Member States to ensure that their websites are accessible to users and, in particular, for people with disabilities, by September 2020. This paper examines the web accessibility of local authority websites in the Republic of Ireland. It provides an evaluation of web and accessibility statement availability, web accessibility, search engine visibility, and social media visibility, using manual and automated methods. Despite the minimum requirements set out in the Web Accessibility Directive, the overwhelming majority of local government websites examined continue to present significant accessibility issues and vary in the form and detail of their accessibility statements.**

***Keywords*—web accessibility; mobile accessibility; accessibility audits; e-government; local government; web accessibility directive; local authorities**

I. INTRODUCTION

In 2021, almost 58% of people in the European Union (EU) aged 16–74 years made use of the internet to interact with public authorities [1]. The ISO define accessibility as "...the extent to which products, systems, services, environments and facilities can be used by people from a population with the widest range of user needs, characteristics and capabilities to achieve identified goals in identified contexts of use, where such contexts include direct use or use supported by assistive technologies." [2]. In scholarly literature, website accessibility is an oft-referenced term but has many meanings. As Krol Zdonek [3] note it may refer to (i) the ability to browse web content comfortably, regardless of physical limitations, (ii) search engine visibility, (iii) social media visibility, and (iv) web availability. A key theme in web accessibility literature is the removal of barriers to access and use online information and services for people with disabilities and the elderly [4][5][6]. While commentators note that the concept of 'disability' is ambiguous, indeterminate, multifarious, political, culturally contingent, multi-dimensional and highly complex [3][5][7], the focus of web accessibility evaluation literature, standards, and legislation has been on visual and auditory disabilities and to a lesser extent cognitive, and motor disabilities.

The legal standing of web accessibility has been debated since the first decade of the worldwide web [4]. In particular, there has been a significant and growing movement to legislate for government websites and those of public sector bodies to meet minimum web accessibility standards resulting in Section 508 of the US Rehabilitation Act Amendments of 1998, Section 20(6) of the UK Equality Act 2010, and most recently the EU Directive on the accessibility of the websites and mobile applications of public sector bodies. These laws typically require public sector websites to meet a set of testable criteria based on the 2010 ADA Standards for Accessible Design and guidelines recommended by the world wide web consortium (W3C).

Over the last two decades, the introduction and ubiquity of the smartphone has significantly changed how the public access online information and services including public sector websites. This is reflected in the Directive (EU) 2016/2102 of the European Parliament and of the Council of 26 October 2016 on the accessibility of the websites and mobile applications of public sector bodies (the Web Accessibility Directive) enacted on 26 October 2016, which became law in Member States on 23 September 2018. The Web Accessibility Directive requires public sector bodies to ensure that their websites and mobile applications are more accessible in particular for people with disabilities. The Web Accessibility Directive specifically requires public sector websites to meet the so-called POUR principles of accessibility i.e. perceivability, operability, understandability, and robustness, and is testable against criteria such as those laid out in the European standard EN 301 549 V1.1.2, which is largely based on the W3C Web Content Accessibility Guidelines (WCAG) 2.0. The Web Accessibility Directive allowed for a phased implementation of measures with all public sector websites to be compliant by 23 September 2020. As a result, there has been a renewed interest by scholars in the web accessibility of both national and local government websites in the EU (see for example [3][8]).

Article 28A of the Irish Constitution recognises the role of local government in providing a forum for the democratic representation of communities and in exercising and performing powers conferred by law. The primary legislative code outlining the structures, powers, functions, and duties of local government in Republic of Ireland is laid out in the Local Government Act 2001 and the Local Government Reform Act 2014. There are currently 31 local authorities in the Republic of Ireland - 26 county councils, three city councils (Cork, Dublin and Galway), and two city and county councils (Limerick and Waterford). The operations of local authorities are also impacted by other legislation. This paper assesses the website accessibility of the 31 local authorities in the Republic of Ireland. The Web Accessibility Directive was transposed in to Irish law through the European Union (Accessibility of Websites and Mobile Applications of Public Sector Bodies) Regulations 2020, which came into force on 23 September 2020. The remainder of this paper will be organised as follows; in Section 2 the data and methods will be presented, Section 3 will discuss the results over four headings (namely website availability, accessibility statements and assistive technologies, website accessibility, search engine visibility, and social media visibility), and finally Section 4 will outline our conclusions.

II. DATA AND METHODS

The study involves all 31 websites of local authorities in the Republic of Ireland. This study examined four aspects of web accessibility, namely: web availability, web accessibility, search engine visibility, and social media visibility. We only focus on websites. Data was collected in December 2022 and January 2023, both manually and using automated tools. Firstly, whether the website uses secure http (HTTPS), data on the availability of a web accessibility policy, the availability of assistive tools on each local government website, and social media presence was manually collected. In addition, search engine accessibility was examined by manually checking whether (a) a robots.txt file blocked search engine crawling, the local authority was displayed in a knowledge panel and whether it was claimed or unclaimed, and (c) as per King & Youngblood [10] whether the county website ranked on the first page of search engine results on Google, Bing, Twitter and Facebook. Secondly, we utilised PowerMapper's OnDemand Suite, a commercial software tool that scans web code against 1,300 standards-based checkpoints including WCAG 2.1, WCAG 2.0, Section 508 (2017), accessible file formats, desktop and browser mobile compatibility, broken links and errors, web standards (including W3C HTML and CSS standards), and Google and Bing SEO best practice guidelines. Thirdly, Google Lighthouse, an open-source, automated tool for improving the quality of web pages, was used to assess both desktop and mobile quality of experience. Finally, the Google Mobile Friendly Test tool was used to test mobile usability. PowerMapper's OnDemand Suite and Google Lighthouse are used widely by private and public sector organisations for accessibility and quality of experience evaluation, and increasingly in scholarly research (see, for example, [3][10][17]).

III. RESULTS AND DISCUSSION

The following section evaluates these websites over four points of discussion, namely; website availability and its adherence to regulations on accessibility statements and assistive technologies, the accessibility of the websites in a number of categories; the search engine visibility, and the social media visibility.

A. Website Availability, Accessibility Statements and Assistive Technologies

With respect to web availability, local authorities in Ireland all have a dedicated website. Over 77% of Irish citizens use a smartphone for private purposes [19] and over 99% of Irish Internet users use a smartphone to access the Internet [20]. As such, mobile usability is an important factor in web availability and accessibility for local authorities. The Google Mobile Friendly Testing tool was used to test usability on smartphones. One local authority blocked Google crawls. Of the other 30 websites, 28 were deemed usable on a smartphone (mobile friendly). HTTPS provides and additional layer of protection to data transferred between users and websites by providing cryptographic security protection for data, authenticating websites using digital certificates, and enabling browser-based security mechanisms [21]. These mechanisms provide protection to web traffic from network attackers and build trust in websites and the web in general. Without HTTPS, any data passed is insecure. Furthermore, if HTTPS is not used search engines will display a warning which may adversely impact trust in the local authority. Only one website in the sample did not use HTTPS. While this suggests high penetration, it is still surprising that there was not full coverage.

Regulation 7 of the European Union (Accessibility of Websites and Mobile Applications of Public Sector Bodies) Regulations 2020 requires an accessibility statement in a required form to be published on local authority websites. While our results found that the requirement to publish an accessibility statement on local authority websites has been generally complied with, the form and detail varies significantly particularly with respect to the accessibility links on local authority homepages. Implementation ranges from detailed accessibility statements to links to empty web pages or external third-party websites. The Web Accessibility Directive and associated regulations do not require local authorities to integrate or implement assistive tools; it is as a 'minimum harmonisation' directive. This means that it only sets out the absolute minimum requirements that must be met by public sector bodies for their websites and mobile applications. Notwithstanding this, for public sector bodies it is reasonable to consider the provision and integration of assistive technologies as best practice. Only eight local authority

TABLE I
LOCAL AUTHORITY WEBSITE AVAILABILITY

Local Authority	Website	HTTPS	Mobile Friendly
Carlow CC	Y	Y	Y
Cavan CC	Y	Y	Y
Clare CC	Y	Y	Y
Cork CiC	Y	Y	Y
Cork CC	Y	Y	Y
Dun Laoghaire-Rathdown CC	Y	Y	Y
Donegal CC	Y	Y	Y
Dublin CiC	Y	Y	Y
Fingal CC	Y	Y	Y
Galway CiC	Y	Y	Y
Galway CC	Y	Y	Y
Kerry CC	Y	Y	Y
Kildare CC	Y	Y	Y
Kilkenny CC	Y	Y	Y
Laois CC	Y	Y	Y
Leitrim CC	Y	Y	Y
Limerick CCC	Y	Y	Y
Longford CC	Y	Y	Y
Louth CC	Y	Y	Y
Mayo CC	Y	Y	Y
Meath CC	Y	Y	Y
Monaghan CC	Y	Y	Y
Offaly CC	Y	N	Y
Roscommon CC	Y	Y	NA
Sligo CC	Y	Y	Y
South Dublin CC	Y	Y	Y
Tipperary CC	Y	Y	Y
Waterford CCC	Y	Y	Y
Westmeath CC	Y	Y	Y
Wexford CC	Y	Y	Y
Wicklow CC	Y	Y	Y

Notes — CC: County Council; CiC: City Council; CCC: City and County Council.

TABLE II
LOCAL AUTHORITY ACCESSIBILITY STATEMENT AND ASSISTIVE TOOL AVAILABILITY.

Local Authority	Statement	Homepage Link	Assistive Tools
Carlow CC	N	N	N
Cavan CC	Y	Y	N
Clare CC	Y	Y	N
Cork CiC	Y	Y	Y
Cork CC	Y	Y	Y
Dun Laoghaire-Rathdown CC	Y	Y	Y
Donegal CC	Y*	Y	N
Dublin CiC	Y	Y	N
Fingal CC	Y	Y	Y
Galway CiC	Y	Y	N
Galway CC	Y	Y	N
Kerry CC	Y	Y	N
Kildare CC	Y	Y	N
Kilkenny CC	N	N	Y
Laois CC	Y	N	N***
Leitrim CC	Y	Y	N
Limerick CCC	Y	N	N
Longford CC	Y	Y	N
Louth CC	Y	Y	N
Mayo CC	Y	Y	N***
Meath CC	Y	N	N
Monaghan CC	Y	Y	Y
Offaly CC	N**	Y	Y
Roscommon CC	Y	Y	N***
Sligo CC	Y	Y	N
South Dublin CC	Y	Y	N
Tipperary CC	Y	Y	N
Waterford CCC	Y	N	N
Westmeath CC	Y	N	N
Wexford CC	N	N	Y
Wicklow CC	Y	Y	N

Notes — CC: County Council; CiC: City Council; CCC: City and County Council. *Links to W3C WAI Guidelines. **Website featured link to webpage however no content was present on target page. ***Accessibility statement references assistive tools but tools were not integrated into website.

websites in the sample featured integrated assistive technologies. Table I summarises our findings by website.

Article 7 of the Web Accessibility Directive requires local authorities to produce an accessibility statement in an accessible format and to be published on the website concerned. 26 county councils had web accessibility statements of some form on their website and 23 featured web accessibility statements of some form on the homepage of their website.

The Web Accessibility Directive also requires accessibility statements to be prepared using the model accessibility statement referred to in Commission Implementing Decision EU 2018/1523. While our results found that the requirement to publish an accessibility statement on a local authority website has been generally complied with, the form and detail varies significantly. For example, one merely provided links to the Access Officer, another linked to the W3C Web Accessibility Initiative (WAI), and one linked to a page containing no content.

The Web Accessibility Directive and associated regulations do not require local authorities to integrate or implement assistive tools. As discussed above, it is a 'minimum harmonisation' directive. Notwithstanding this, for public sector bodies it is reasonable to consider the provision and integration of assistive technologies as best practice. Only eight local authority websites in the sample featured integrated assistive technologies; a further three referenced recommended assistive technologies. Three such technologies were prevalent - Recite Me (6), Reachdeck (3), and Browse Aloud (2). Table II summarises our findings by website.

B. Website Accessibility

PowerMapper's OnDemand Suite was used to evaluate five categories of standards-based checkpoints:

- Errors - quality issues including broken links, server configuration problems, script errors and issues with Internet RFCs;
- Accessibility issues - compliance with WCAG 2.1 and Section 508 (2017);
- Compatibility issues - browser-specific content, functionality, layout or performance problems;
- Standards issues - validation that pages meet W3C HTML/XHTML and CSS standards and identification of issues related to W3C deprecated features; and,
- Usability issues - general usability issues based on Usability.gov guidelines, W3C Best Practices, and readability.

In addition, to identifying the number of pages with issues, PowerMapper provides a benchmark against websites in their test database. Sites are designated worse or better. Overall, 29 local authority websites could be scanned; two blocked remote scanning. Our results also suggest that the local authorities in the sample had significant volumes of pages on their websites featuring quality issues and errors, as well as browser incompatibility and non-compliance with accessibility, technical web standards and usability guidelines. All 29 websites performed worse than the PowerMapper benchmark. Overall, the sample websites performed better than the benchmark in only one category, Errors, where 21 websites performed better than the benchmark. Only one website in the sample performed better than the Powermapper benchmark for each of accessibility and usability. Table III summarises our findings by website.

Google Lighthouse was used to measure the quality of experience of each website across three measures - performance, accessibility, and best practice - for both mobile and desktop users. Performance measures how well a given page is optimised for users to be able to see and interact with page content. Accessibility assesses the extent to which all users can access content and navigate a given website effectively. Best practices assess the underlying code health of a given website against best practice. Google Lighthouse score ranges are: 0 to 49 (red): Poor; 50 to 89 (orange): Needs Improvement; and 90 to 100 (green): Good. Table IV presents the results from Google Lighthouse analysis. Our results suggest while local authority websites in the sample are usable on smartphones, performance, accessibility, and alignment with best practices for mobile use varies significantly with most websites requiring significant improvements. Desktop results were significantly better than those for mobile suggesting that the websites were primarily designed for desktop users. Notwithstanding this, there is clear room for improvement. Table V summarises our results.

C. Search Engine Visibility

Search engine visibility are not required under legislation although they play an important role in information accessibility and discoverability. As per King & Youngblood [9] we manually assessed whether each local authority website ranked on the first page of search engine results on Google and Bing. In all cases, the local government website featured in the first search engine results page. Knowledge panels give websites more exposure as they occupy more space in a search engine results page, is more understandable and provides better usability by giving faster access to important information and links. In each case, a knowledge panel was displayed for each local authority however in 11 cases, the knowledge panel had not been claimed thereby limiting the range and timeliness of data that could be displayed. If a website uses a robots.txt file to limit crawling, its URL can still appear in search results but the search result will not have a description, non-HTML files will be excluded, and rich results will not display. As such, it can impact website accessibility and usability. Only three websites blocked search engine crawling. Table VI summarises our findings by website.

OnDemand Suite was also used to evaluate whether a given website met Google, Bing and Yahoo! search guidelines, robots.txt guidelines, and search best practices. Again, two websites blocked scans of their website. Of the remaining 29, only two websites performed better than the PowerMapper benchmark in the search category. Furthermore, Google Lighthouse was used to assess how well a given website is optimised for search engines. Again, score ranges are: 0 to 49 (red): Poor; 50 to 89 (orange): Needs Improvement; and 90 to 100 (green): Good. Generally speaking, Google Lighthouse results for SEO were relatively high for both mobile and desktop with an average score of 84 for both. Table VII summarises our findings by website.

D. Social media visibility

In Europe, on average 58% of the individuals participated in online social networking sites in 2022 [23]. While statistics are not available for Ireland for 2022, historically Irish social media use has been higher than the EU average [24]. 30 of the websites provided links to at least one social networking sites on their home page and 28 provided links to two or more social networking sites. Twitter (30) and Facebook (208) were the most prevalent. Table VIII summarises our findings by website. In addition, we completed the same manual assessment on social media search engine results on Facebook and Twitter. All local authorities featured on the first (extended) search engine results page for Twitter and 29 local authorities featured on the first search engine results page on Facebook.

IV. CONCLUSIONS

Policymakers and legislators have made significant efforts to ensure that minimum standards are met for website accessibility. Our findings suggest that in Ireland, despite these efforts, there are some key issues to be addressed in nearly all local authority websites. Many of these issues are neither difficult to implement nor costly. As demonstrated from this paper, the identification of issues at a page level can be achieved using free and commercial off-the-shelf tools. Further research is required to identify the specific barriers to achieving and maintaining web accessibility.

Regulation 8 of the European Union (Accessibility of Websites and Mobile Applications of Public Sector Bodies) Regulations 2020 names the National Disability Authority as the monitoring body. Although testing different samples with some overlap, our findings are consistent with their 2021 Monitoring Report (see [21]). This suggests that greater commitment to accessibility is required by public sector bodies but also that the monitoring body requires more effective enforcement procedures (including penalties). Local authorities

TABLE III
LOCAL AUTHORITY ONDEMAND SUITE SCAN RESULTS.

Local Authority	Pages Scanned	Quality Issues	Errors	Accessibility	Compatibility	Standards	Usability	Overall	Errors	Accessibility	Compatibility	Standards	Usability
Carlow CC	529	301	8	277	28	59	66	Worse	Better	Worse	Better	Better	Better
Cavan CC	529	467	2	465	431	467	467	Worse	Better	Worse	Worse	Worse	Worse
Clare CC	527	317	21	315	305	304	304	Worse	Better	Worse	Worse	Worse	Worse
Cork CiC	526	373	68	368	372	370	368	Worse	Better	Worse	Worse	Worse	Worse
Cork CC	528	337	314	328	322	316	316	Worse	Worse	Worse	Worse	Worse	Worse
Dun Laoghaire-Rathdown CC	530	239	11	211	228	218	180	Worse	Better	Worse	Worse	Worse	Worse
Donegal CC	NA	NA	NA	NA	NA	NA	NA	NA	NA	NA	NA	NA	NA
Dublin CiC	527	365	182	358	359	356	357	Worse	Worse	Worse	Worse	Worse	Worse
Fingal CC	521	319	308	309	6	310	314	Worse	Worse	Worse	Better	Worse	Worse
Galway CiC	520	339	334	332	9	295	335	Worse	Worse	Worse	Better	Worse	Worse
Galway CC	524	343	83	338	47	305	305	Worse	Better	Worse	Worse	Worse	Worse
Kerry CC	519	323	11	306	318	305	150	Worse	Better	Worse	Worse	Worse	Worse
Kildare CC	525	246	15	223	44	223	225	Worse	Better	Worse	Worse	Worse	Worse
Kilkenny CC	523	330	4	321	320	315	315	Worse	Better	Worse	Worse	Worse	Worse
	464	190	169	178	180	172	176	Worse	Worse	Worse	Worse	Worse	Worse
Leitrim CC	530	482	6	474	478	477	478	Worse	Better	Worse	Worse	Worse	Worse
Limerick CCC	528	202	194	196	200	198	199	Worse	Worse	Worse	Worse	Worse	Worse
Longford CC	519	325	29	320	26	316	319	Worse	Better	Worse	Better	Worse	Worse
Louth CC	530	491	108	482	491	487	487	Worse	Worse	Worse	Worse	Worse	Worse
Mayo CC	529	385	382	381	321	382	383	Worse	Worse	Worse	Worse	Worse	Worse
Meath CC	504	356	6	239	356	355	356	Worse	Better	Worse	Worse	Worse	Worse
Monaghan CC	527	446	7	443	466	454	453	Worse	Better	Worse	Worse	Worse	Worse
Offaly CC	525	487	5	474	487	479	482	Worse	Better	Worse	Worse	Worse	Worse
Roscommon CC	NA	NA	NA	NA	NA	NA	NA	NA	NA	NA	NA	NA	NA
Sligo CC	520	284	26	273	279	273	274	Worse	Better	Worse	Worse	Worse	Worse
South Dublin CC	528	458	3	454	458	457	456	Worse	Better	Worse	Worse	Worse	Worse
Tipperary CC	517	335	2	320	15	322	329	Worse	Better	Worse	Better	Worse	Worse
Waterford CCC	527	349	29	50	58	336	338	Worse	Better	Better	Worse	Worse	Worse
Westmeath CC	530	353	4	348	4	192	351	Worse	Better	Worse	Better	Worse	Worse
Wexford CC	528	338	33	334	12	319	321	Worse	Better	Worse	Better	Worse	Worse
Wicklow CC	529	495	30	480	19	486	488	Worse	Better	Worse	Better	Worse	Worse

Notes — CC: County Council; CiC: City Council; CCC: City and County Council

TABLE III
LOCAL AUTHORITY ONDEMAND SUITE SCAN RESULTS.

Local Authority	Pages Scanned	Quality Issues	Errors	Accessibility	Compatibility	Standards	Usability	Overall	Errors	Accessibility	Compatibility	Standards	Usability
Carlow CC	529	301	8	277	28	59	66	Worse	Better	Worse	Better	Better	Better
Cavan CC	529	467	2	465	431	467	467	Worse	Better	Worse	Worse	Worse	Worse
Clare CC	527	317	21	315	305	304	304	Worse	Better	Worse	Worse	Worse	Worse
Cork CiC	526	373	68	368	372	370	368	Worse	Better	Worse	Worse	Worse	Worse
Cork CC	528	337	314	328	322	316	316	Worse	Worse	Worse	Worse	Worse	Worse
Dun Laoghaire-Rathdown CC	530	239	11	211	228	218	180	Worse	Better	Worse	Worse	Worse	Worse
Donegal CC	NA	NA	NA	NA	NA	NA	NA	NA	NA	NA	NA	NA	NA
Dublin CiC	527	365	182	358	359	356	357	Worse	Worse	Worse	Worse	Worse	Worse
Fingal CC	521	319	308	309	6	310	314	Worse	Worse	Worse	Better	Worse	Worse
Galway CiC	520	339	334	332	9	295	335	Worse	Worse	Worse	Better	Worse	Worse
Galway CC	524	343	83	338	47	305	305	Worse	Better	Worse	Worse	Worse	Worse
Kerry CC	519	323	11	306	318	305	150	Worse	Better	Worse	Worse	Worse	Worse
Kildare CC	525	246	15	223	44	223	225	Worse	Better	Worse	Worse	Worse	Worse
Kilkenny CC	523	330	4	321	320	315	315	Worse	Better	Worse	Worse	Worse	Worse
Laois CC	464	190	169	178	180	172	176	Worse	Worse	Worse	Worse	Worse	Worse
Leitrim CC	530	482	6	474	478	477	478	Worse	Better	Worse	Worse	Worse	Worse
Limerick CCC	528	202	194	196	200	198	199	Worse	Worse	Worse	Worse	Worse	Worse
Longford CC	519	325	29	320	26	316	319	Worse	Better	Worse	Better	Worse	Worse
Louth CC	530	491	108	482	491	487	487	Worse	Worse	Worse	Worse	Worse	Worse
Mayo CC	529	385	382	381	321	382	383	Worse	Worse	Worse	Worse	Worse	Worse
Meath CC	504	356	6	239	356	355	356	Worse	Better	Worse	Worse	Worse	Worse
Monaghan CC	527	446	7	443	466	454	453	Worse	Better	Worse	Worse	Worse	Worse
Offaly CC	525	487	5	474	487	479	482	Worse	Better	Worse	Worse	Worse	Worse
Roscommon CC	NA	NA	NA	NA	NA	NA	NA	NA	NA	NA	NA	NA	NA
Sligo CC	520	284	26	273	279	273	274	Worse	Better	Worse	Worse	Worse	Worse
South Dublin CC	528	458	3	454	458	457	456	Worse	Better	Worse	Worse	Worse	Worse
Tipperary CC	517	335	2	320	15	322	329	Worse	Better	Worse	Better	Worse	Worse
Waterford CCC	527	349	29	50	58	336	338	Worse	Better	Better	Worse	Worse	Worse
Westmeath CC	530	353	4	348	4	192	351	Worse	Better	Worse	Better	Worse	Worse
Wexford CC	528	338	33	334	12	319	321	Worse	Better	Worse	Better	Worse	Worse
Wicklow CC	529	495	30	480	19	486	488	Worse	Better	Worse	Better	Worse	Worse

Notes — CC: County Council; CiC: City Council; CCC: City and County Council.

TABLE IV
GOOGLE MOBILE FRIENDLY AND GOOGLE LIGHTHOUSE PERFORMANCE RESULTS

County Council	Mobile Friendly	Mobile Performance	Mobile Accessibility	Mobile Best Practices	Desktop Performance	Desktop Accessibility	Desktop Best Practices
Carlow CC	Usable	40	88	67	80	88	75
Cavan CC	Usable	76	99	92	94	99	92
Clare CC	Usable	76	99	92	94	99	92
Cork CiC	Usable	50	90	100	76	90	100
Cork CC	Usable	42	81	75	91	73	67
Dun Laoghaire-Rathdown CC	Usable	44	89	92	64	89	92
Donegal CC	Usable	43	100	42	89	93	42
Dublin CiC	Usable	NA	NA	NA	63	100	92
Fingal CC	Usable	72	90	83	96	90	92
Galway CiC	Usable	75	83	83	84	83	83
Galway CC	Usable	58	83	75	88	83	83
Kerry CC	Usable	50	83	83	76	87	83
Kildare CC	Usable	24	81	67	50	84	75
Kilkenny CC	Usable	70	96	92	96	96	92
Laois CC	Usable	39	91	67	70	88	75
Leitrim CC	NA	42	78	NA	74	83	NA
Limerick CCC	Usable	38	89	83	86	89	83
Longford CC	Usable	12	77	75	29	85	75
Louth CC	NA	30	84	NA	85	86	NA
Mayo CC	Usable	45	100	83	99	99	83
Meath CC	Usable	91	100	100	97	100	100
Monaghan CC	Usable	12	86	75	24	86	83
Offaly CC	Usable	12	84	75	57	77	75
Roscommon CC	NA	NA	NA	NA	NA	NA	NA
Sligo CC	Usable	43	99	83	73	99	83
South Dublin CC	Usable	8	100	67	60	100	75
Tipperary CC	Usable	69	88	83	92	86	92
Waterford CCC	Usable	67	93	67	96	93	67
Westmeath CC	Usable	70	98	83	92	98	92
Wexford CC	Usable	60	90	83	90	84	92
Wicklow CC	Usable	26	92	83	78	84	83

Notes — CC: County Council; CiC: City Council; CCC: City and County Council.

should be the leaders in ensuring a more accessible Internet in their community. While much has been done, there would seem to be a lot more to do.

ACKNOWLEDGMENT

This research was partially funded by the Irish Department of Rural and Community Development with additional support from .IE, the official registry of .ie domain names.

REFERENCES

[1] Eurostat, Digital society statistics at regional level. May 2022.

[2] ISO, ISO 9241-11:2018 - Ergonomics of human-system interaction — Part 11: Usability: Definitions and concepts. 2018.

[3] K. Krol and D. Zdonek, "Local Government Website Accessibility—Evidence from Poland", Administrative Sciences, Mar 31; vol.10, no. 2, pp.:22, 2020.

[4] C. Peters and D. A. Bradbard, "Web accessibility: an introduction and ethical implications", Journal of Information, Communication and Ethics in Society, May 4, 2010.

[5] S. Lewthwaite, "Web accessibility standards and disability: developing critical perspectives on accessibility", Disability and Rehabilitation, Aug 1, vol. 36, no. 16, pp.1375 - 83, 2014.

[6] H. Y. Abuaddous, M. Z. Jali, and N. Basir, "Web accessibility challenges", International Journal of Advanced Computer Science and Applications (IJACSA), 2016.

[7] S. Linton, "Claiming disability: Knowledge and identity", NyU Press; 1998.

[8] S. Valtolina and D. Fratus, "Local Government Websites Accessibility: Evaluation and Findings from Italy", Digital Government Research and Practice, Oct 14, vol. 14, no. 3, pp. 1 - 6, 2022.

[9] S. Kanta, "Insights with PowerMapper and R: An exploratory data analysis of US Government website accessibility scans," Proceedings of the 2018 ICT Accessibility Testing Symposium: Mobile Testing, Nov 7, vol. 508, pp. 65-72, 2018.

[10] B. A. King and N. E. Youngblood, "E-government in Alabama: An analysis of county voting and election website content, usability, accessibility, and mobile readiness," Government Information Quarterly, Oct 1, vol. 33, no. 4, pp. 715-26, 2016.

[11] I. N. Sodhar, H. Bhanbhro, and Z. H. Amur, "Evaluation of web accessibility of engineering university websites of Pakistan through online tools," IJCSNS, Dec; vol.19, no.12, pp. 85-90, 2019.

[12] S. M. Baule, "Evaluating the accessibility of special education cooperative websites for individuals with disabilities," TechTrends, Jan; vol. 64, no. 1, pp.50-6, 2020.

[13] N. Angraini, M. J. Putra, and N. Hakiem, "Development of an Islamic Higher Education Institution Tracer Study Information System and It's Performance Analysis using ISO/IEC 25010," 2019 7th International Conference on Cyber and IT Service Management (CITSM), Nov 6, vol. 7, pp. 1-6). IEEE, 2019.

[14] D. Saif, C. H. Lung, and A. Matrawy, "An early benchmark of quality of experience between HTTP/2 and HTTP/3 using lighthouse," ICC 2021-IEEE International Conference on Communications, Jun 14, pp. 1-6, IEEE, 2021.

[15] S. Gopinath, V. Senthooran, N. Lojenaa, and T. Kartheeswaran, "Usability and accessibility analysis of selected government websites in Sri Lanka," 2016 IEEE Region 10 Symposium (TENSYMP), May 9, pp. 394-398, IEEE, 2016.

[16] M. Bilal, Z. Yu, S. Song, and C. Wang, "Evaluate accessibility and usability issues of particular China and Pakistan government websites," 2019 2nd International Conference on Artificial Intelligence and Big Data (ICAIBD), May 25, pp. 316-322, IEEE, 2019.

[17] S. Ganapati, "Using mobile apps in government. Washington DC," IBM Center for The Business of Government, 2015.

[18] K. Roumeliotis and N. D. Tselikas, "Evaluating Progressive Web App Accessibility for People with Disabilities," Network, Jun, vol. 2, no. 2, pp. 350-69, 2022.

[19] S. Gibney and T. McCarthy, "Profile of smartphone ownership and use in Ireland," Government of Ireland. 2020.

[20] Central Statistics Office, "Internet Coverage and Usage in Ireland 2021," 2021.

[21] A. P. Felt, R. Barnes, A. King, C. Palmer, C. Bentzel, and P. Tabriz, "Measuring HTTPS adoption on the web," 26th USENIX Security Symposium (USENIX Security 17), pp. 1323-1338, 2017.

[22] National Disability Authority, "Ireland's Monitoring Report for the EU Web Accessibility Directive," 2021.

[23] Eurostat, "EU regions: how did people use the internet in 2022?" 2022.

[24] Eurostat, "EU regions: how did people use the internet in 2021?" 2022.

TABLE V
GOOGLE LIGHTHOUSE ASSESSMENT SCORES

Metric	Poor	Needs Improvement	Good	NA	Total
Mobile Performance	16	12	1	2	31
Mobile Accessibility	0	14	15	2	31
Mobile Best Practices	1	20	6	4	31
Desktop Performance	2	17	11	1	31
Desktop Accessibility	0	17	13	1	31
Desktop Best Practices	1	16	11	3	31

TABLE VI
LOCAL AUTHORITY WEBSITE SEARCH ENGINE VISIBILITY MANUAL EVALUATION.

Local Authority	Robots.txt	Google SERP1	Bing SERP1	Knowledge Panel
Carlow CC	N	Y	Y	Claimed
Cavan CC	N	Y	Y	Claimed
Clare CC	N	Y	Y	Claimed
Cork CiC	N	Y	Y	Unclaimed
Cork CC	N	Y	Y	Claimed
Dun Laoghaire-Rathdown CC	N	Y	Y	Claimed
Donegal CC	N	Y	Y	Claimed
Dublin CiC	N	Y	Y	Claimed
Fingal CC	N	Y	Y	Unclaimed
Galway CC	N	Y	Y	Claimed
Galway CiC	N	Y	Y	Unclaimed
Kerry CC	N	Y	Y	Claimed
Kildare CC	N	Y	Y	Unclaimed
Kilkenny CC	N	Y	Y	Claimed
Laois CC	N	Y	Y	Claimed
Leitrim CC	Y	Y	Y	Claimed
Limerick CCC	N	Y	Y	Unclaimed
Longford CC	N	Y	Y	Claimed
Louth CC	Y	Y	Y	Claimed
Mayo CC	N	Y	Y	Claimed
Meath CC	N	Y	Y	Claimed
Monaghan CC	N	Y	Y	Unclaimed
Offaly CC	N	Y	Y	Claimed
Roscommon CC	Y	Y	Y	Claimed
Sligo CC	N	Y	Y	Unclaimed
South Dublin CC	N	Y	Y	Unclaimed
Tipperary CC	N	Y	Y	Unclaimed
Waterford CCC	N	Y	Y	Claimed
Westmeath CC	N	Y	Y	Claimed
Wexford CC	N	Y	Y	Unclaimed
Wicklow CC	N	Y	Y	Unclaimed

Notes — CC: County Council; CiC: City Council; CCC: City and County Council.

TABLE VII
LOCAL AUTHORITY AUTOMATED SEARCH ENGINE VISIBILITY RATINGS BY WEBSITE

County Council	Google Lighthouse		Google Lighthouse		OnDemand Suite	
	Mobile SEO	*Desktop SEO*	*Mobile SEO*	*Desktop SEO*	*Pages with Search Issues*	*Benchmark*
Carlow CC	84	83	Needs Improvement	Needs Improvement	28	Better
Cavan CC	100	100	Good	Good	347	Worse
Clare CC	100	100	Good	Good	252	Worse
Cork CiC	83	83	Needs Improvement	Needs Improvement	267	Worse
Cork CC	85	82	Needs Improvement	Needs Improvement	241	Worse
Dun Laoghaire-Rathdown CC	77	73	Needs Improvement	Needs Improvement	191	Worse
Donegal CC	88	90	Needs Improvement	Good	NA	NA
Dublin CiC	NA	79	NA	Needs Improvement	142	Worse
Fingal CC	84	83	Needs Improvement	Needs Improvement	228	Worse
Galway CC	74	73	Needs Improvement	Needs Improvement	43	Worse
Galway CiC	75	73	Needs Improvement	Needs Improvement	107	Worse
Kerry CC	87	92	Needs Improvement	Good	299	Worse
Kildare CC	89	90	Needs Improvement	Good	43	Better
Kilkenny CC	88	91	Needs Improvement	Good	312	Worse
Laois CC	75	73	Needs Improvement	Needs Improvement	107	Worse
Leitrim CC	NA	NA	NA	NA	330	Worse
Limerick CCC	93	92	Good	Good	151	Worse
Longford CC	97	100	Good	Good	117	Worse
Louth CC	81	82	Needs Improvement	Needs Improvement	258	Worse
Mayo CC	92	92	Good	Good	373	Worse
Meath CC	92	92	Good	Good	336	Worse
Monaghan CC	69	67	Needs Improvement	Needs Improvement	441	Worse
Offaly CC	82	82	Needs Improvement	Needs Improvement	189	Worse
Roscommon CC	NA	NA	NA	NA	NA	NA
Sligo CC	83	80	Needs Improvement	Needs Improvement	266	Worse
South Dublin CC	89	91	Needs Improvement	Good	454	Worse
Tipperary CC	66	64	Needs Improvement	Needs Improvement	201	Worse
Waterford CCC	87	90	Needs Improvement	Good	282	Worse
Westmeath CC	100	100	Good	Good	348	Worse
Wexford CC	84	83	Needs Improvement	Needs Improvement	318	Worse
Wicklow CC	82	73	Needs Improvement	Needs Improvement	472	Worse

Notes — CC: County Council; CiC: City Council; CCC: City and County Council

TABLE VIII
SOCIAL MEDIA PRESENCE ON LOCAL AUTHORITY WEBSITE HOMEPAGE.

County Council	Total SNS	Twitter	Facebook	LinkedIn	Instagram	Youtube	Pinterest	Flickr	Vimeo
Carlow CC	4	1	1	0	0	0	1	1	0
Cavan CC	5	1	1	1	1	1	0	0	0
Clare CC	4	1	1	0	1	1	0	0	0
Cork CiC	5	1	1	1	1	1	0	0	0
Cork CC	5	1	1	1	1	1	0	0	0
Dun Laoghaire-Rathdown CC	4	1	1	0	1	1	0	0	0
Donegal CC	4	1	1	1	0	1	0	0	0
Dublin CiC	3	1	1	0	1	0	0	0	0
Fingal CC	5	1	1	1	1	1	0	0	0
Galway CC	2	1	1	0	0	0	0	0	0
Galway CiC	2	1	1	0	0	0	0	0	0
Kerry CC	3	1	1	0	0	1	0	0	0
Kildare CC	5	1	1	0	1	1	0	0	1
Kilkenny CC	4	1	1	0	1	1	0	0	0
Laois CC	2	1	1	0	0	0	0	0	0
Leitrim CC	3	1	1	0	1	0	0	0	0
Limerick CCC	4	1	1	0	1	1	0	0	0
Longford CC	5	1	1	0	1	1	0	1	0
Louth CC	1	1	0	0	0	0	0	0	0
Mayo CC	5	1	1	1	1	1	0	0	0
Meath CC	4	1	1	1	0	1	0	0	0
Mo0ghan CC	0	0	0	0	0	0	0	0	0
Offaly CC	4	1	1	1	1	0	0	0	0
Roscommon CC	2	1	1	0	0	0	0	0	0
South Dublin CC	4	1	1	0	1	1	0	0	0
Sligo CC	5	1	1	1	1	1	0	0	0
Tipperary CC	3	1	1	0	1	0	0	0	0
Waterford CCC	4	1	1	1	0	1	0	0	0
Westmeath CC	3	1	1	0	1	0	0	0	0
Wexford CC	1	1	0	0	0	0	0	0	0
Wicklow CC	3	1	1	0	1	0	0	0	0
Frequency	NA	30	28	10	19	17	1	2	1

Notes — CC: County Council; CiC: City Council; CCC: City and County Council

The Coloniality of Accessibility Links

From Universal Design to a Decolonial Model of (Dis)ability

Lorenzo Dalvit
School of Journalism and Media Studies
Rhodes University
Makhanda, South Africa
e-mail: l.dalvit@ru.ac.za

Abstract—**Accessibility links are an established tool for the digital inclusion of users with disabilities. In this paper, the theoretical lens of coloniality is employed to problematise the role of accessibility links as potentially contributing to entrenching offline classifications and hierarchies, leading to a separate and sometimes inferior user experience. Practical examples are used to highlight three key issues. In conclusion, there is an argument for the need for a decolonial model, to be developed in a dedicated future publication.**

Keywords- coloniality; (dis)ability; accessibility links; universal design; digital inclusion.

I. Introduction

Within decolonial scholarship, the term coloniality refers to the persistent legacy of marginalisation, oppression and exploitation of former colonial subjects long after the end of historical colonialism. Originally coined by Peruvian Sociologist Annibal Quijano to problematise global power relationships [1], uses of the term have been extended to explore issues of race [2], gender [3], citizenship [4] and others, including disability [5][6]. It should be noted that, unlike other terms, the latter does not refer to a dimension of diversity encompassing both privileged and disadvantaged categories (e.g., males and females with regard to gender), but rather signal a deviation from the "norm" [7]. For this reason, wordings such as (dis)ability are preferable. In this paper, I reflect on accessibility links to highlight how coloniality of (dis)ability is reproduced in the online domain. While extensive literature in the field of Human-Computer Interactions exists concerning the inclusion of people with disabilities [8], questions remain as to *how* such users are included. In advancing a decolonial perspective, I highlight the persistent legacy of accessibility as an afterthought, best effort and accommodation rather than truly empowering and liberating. In this paper, I discuss the link between accessibility and coloniality and highlight three key issues.

II. Accessibility Links and Coloniality

Accessibility links are links, often found at the very top of a Web page, which redirect a user with a disability to a specific section, to additional information or to a more accessible version of the page. If not explicitly mandated, they are strongly recommended as an expression of adherence to sound and inclusive design principles [8]. Accessibility links reflect established theoretical understandings of disability [9]. In terms of the medical model, they can be understood as a remedial strategy to provide impaired users with a minimal level of functionality. In terms of the social model, they can be understood as an attempt to remove barriers to access and enable digital inclusion. The latter approach is informed by the principle of universal access by design, i.e., as is the case with new buildings in many western countries [10], Web pages should be conceptualised keeping the needs of a wide range of diverse users in mind and avoid reproducing social forms of discrimination. Both models fail to tackle the existence of (dis)ability as a discrete category or, for that matter, a hierarchical relationship between able and (dis)abled persons, key concerns in decolonial scholarship [11]. Consistent with a critique of the rights-based approach as a form of coloniality [12], formal compliance with accessibility principles does not ensure and may in fact hamper an equitable user experience. Accessibility links represent an example of how artefacts often designed by and for able bodies remain the product of oversimplifications based on formalised users and use scenarios which cannot capture the complexity and nuances of the disability experience in real life. Focusing on a set of purposively selected Web pages, I advocate for a decolonial model of disability by highlighting three issues inherent to current approaches.

III. Issues with Accessibility

The first issue explored in this study is that accessibility links do not always work. Whether this is due to technical problems (e.g., browser compatibility) or human factors (e.g., oversight or non-implementation), accessibility solutions need to be reliable in order to be effective. Taking [13] as an example, even an association with a progressive and inclusive digital media focus can feature a broken "skip to main content" link as tested with Firefox on Ubuntu Linux 20.04.

The second issue concerns quality of experience. Reduced functionality or lack of some key features seems to be considered an acceptable trade-off in the case of users with disabilities. While the provision of alternative and simplified versions of inaccessible webpages seems somewhat dated [14][15], even a health-focused website such as [16] admits to some parts of its site being inaccessible.

The third issue is that accessibility features often entail additional work on the part of the user, e.g., familiarising oneself with page or service-specific features like shortcuts, screen readers, navigation strategies etc., or providing feedback and suggestions for improvement. The most popular website in the world, Google.com, provides an example. Apart from a (functioning) "skip to main content", the other two accessibility links point to separate "accessibility help" and "accessibility feedback" pages. A very rough but conservative estimate based on the number of unique users and percentage of screen reader users in the US, Walsh and Steele [17][18] suggest that potential users could spend a combined 3 million hours or more just to read the help page. Waste of time is recognised as one of the main sources of frustration for screen reader users [19]. While Fuchs [20] recognises free digital labour as a form of capitalist exploitation, Couldry and Mejias [21] highlight the asymmetric and coercive character of digital power relationships as a new form of colonialism.

IV. Conclusion

In summary, though no doubt useful and informed by noble intentions, in some cases, accessibility links reflect power relationships and world views shaped by coloniality in three fundamental ways. Firstly, decisions remain firmly in the hands of people without disabilities with relatively little recourse. Secondly, inclusion is achieved through a separate and often inferior experience. Thirdly, an additional burden in terms of limited features, frustration and extra learning is normalised for people with disabilities. While an exhaustive articulation of a decolonial model of digital inclusion goes beyond the scope of the present paper, it is important to problematise accessibility links as potential contributors to users with disabilities' permanent state of dependency, ghettoisation and suffering, which are the hallmarks of the Global South as a shared subaltern condition rather than a geographical entity.

Acknowledgement

This work is based on the research supported by the National Research Foundation of South Africa (Grant Numbers: 137986)

References

[1] A. Quijano, "Coloniality and modernity/rationality," vol. 21, no. 2–3, pp. 168–178, 2007.

[2] N. Maldonado-Torres, "On the coloniality of being: Contributions to the development of a concept," vol. 21, no. 2–3, pp. 240–270, 2007.

[3] M. Lugones, The coloniality of gender. Springer, 2016.

[4] M. Boatcă and J. Roth, "Unequal and gendered: Notes on the coloniality of citizenship," vol. 64, no. 2, pp. 191–212, 2016.

[5] S. Grech, "Disability and the majority world: A neocolonial approach," pp. 52–69, 2012.

[6] T. P. Dirth and G. A. Adams, "Decolonial theory and disability studies: On the modernity/coloniality of ability.," 2019.

[7] S. Schalk, Resisting erasure: Reading (dis) ability and race in speculative media. Routledge, 2019, pp. 137–146.

[8] J. Abascal and C. Nicolle, "Moving towards inclusive design guidelines for socially and ethically aware HCI," vol. 17, no. 5, pp. 484–505, 2005.

[9] C. Barnes, Understanding the social model of disability: Past, present and future. Routledge, 2019, pp. 14–31.

[10] J. Boys, Doing disability differently: An alternative handbook on architecture, dis/ability and designing for everyday life. Routledge, 2014.

[11] B. de Sousa Santos, "Public sphere and epistemologies of the South," vol. 37, no. 1, pp. 43–67, 2012.

[12] N. Maldonado-Torres, "On the coloniality of human rights," no. 114, pp. 117–136, 2017.

[13] International Association for Media and Communication Research (IAMCR), [Online]. Available from: https://iamcr.org/#main-content. Accessed on 28 March 2023.

[14] D. Sloan, M. Rowan, P. Booth, and P. Gregor, "Ensuring the provision of accessible digital resources," vol. 25, no. 3, pp. 203–216, 2000.

[15] F. Pühretmair, "It's time to make eTourism accessible," 2004, pp. 272–279.

[16] National Health Service (NHS), "Accessibility statement." [Online]. Available from: https://www.nhs.uk/accessibility-statement/. Accessed on 28 March 2023.

[17] S. Walsh, "50 Google Search Statistics & Facts," [Online]. Available from: https://www.semrush.com/blog/google-search-statistics/. Accessed on 28 March 2023.

[18] N. Steele, "Percentage of screen readers users in USA?" [Online]. Available from: https://ux.stackexchange.com/questions/57340/percentage-of-screen-readers-users-in-usa . Accessed on 28 March 2023.

[19] J. Lazar, A. Allen, J. Kleinman, and C. Malarkey, "What frustrates screen reader users on the web: A study of 100 blind users," vol. 22, no. 3, pp. 247–269, 2007.

[20] C. Fuchs, Digital labour and Karl Marx. Routledge, 2014.

[21] N. Couldry and U. A. Mejias, "Data colonialism: Rethinking big data's relation to the contemporary subject," vol. 20, no. 4, pp. 336–349, 2019.

Wine Live Label: A Consumer-Oriented Augmented Reality Design for Wine Labeling

Georgios Lappas
Communication and Digital Media Department,
University of Western Macedonia
Kastoria, Greece
Email: glappas@uowm.gr

Alexandros Kleftodimos
Communication and Digital Media Department,
University of Western Macedonia
Kastoria, Greece
Email: akleftodimos@uowm.gr

Michalis Vrigkas
Communication and Digital Media Department,
University of Western Macedonia
Kastoria, Greece
Email: mvrigkas@uowm.gr

Amalia Triantafyllidou
Communication and Digital Media Department,
University of Western Macedonia
Kastoria, Greece
Email: atriantafylidou@uowm.gr

***Abstract*— Augmented Reality (AR) technologies are emerging technologies that may develop new consumer-oriented devices and services to provide new types of economic activities and business models. In this work, AR technology is used in the marketing sector of the wine industry by creating innovative consumer-oriented experience with augmented "live" wine labels. Starting from the idea of creating an AR experience for wine products, an AR expert designs the AR experience, develops the AR application and the application is distributed to the users with the use of various platforms where the user can interact with the wine label on a whole new level by creating new digital products of wine "live" labels. The purpose of the present study is to examine the impact of AR smartphone applications embedded in wine labels on consumers' experience and their subsequent perceptions and intentions A consumer-oriented approach is used to evaluate the wine-label AR mobile application by examining its impact on consumer experience dimensions, satisfaction, and re-usage intentions towards the application, as well as attitude and purchase intentions towards the wine product. Results found the increase of respondents' satisfaction with the application and in turn help them form positive attitudes and purchase intentions for the wine. This indicates that AR technologies may provide new business models in the marketing sector of food and beverages to enhance user experience, develop positive attitude of costumers to the products and increase purchase intentions towards the products.**

Keywords: Augmented Reality; Wine labels; Digital Marketing; Consumer experience.

I. Introduction

Augmented Reality (AR) technologies as well as Virtual Reality (VR) and Mixed Reality (MR) technologies are constantly gaining ground today in various fields of communication such as entertainment, education, information, marketing, and advertising but also in other fields such as industrial product design and medicine. These technologies could not leave the food and drink industry unaffected, where a system of augmented reality can be used to enable the combination or enhancement of the real world with digital objects or digital information for extending print information with interactive digital objects. Wine companies nowadays are increasingly utilizing AR technologies to promote their products. With the help of augmented-reality technology, wineries are able to provide rich digital content to their customers through videos, 2D/3D animations, photos, and text to enhance their experience [1].

AR technologies can support marketing and promotional activities of companies and in turn foster the relationships of consumers with the brands [2]. Marketers are utilizing these technologies to provide augmented and immersive content for a product/service using a physical background [3]. AR technologies can offer exceptional experiences to consumers since they aim at enhancing consumers' interactions with the product/service [4]. Herein, consumer experience is a multidimensional construct [5] that encapsulates various dimensions such as hedonism-entertainment, flow, escapism, learning, challenge, socialization, and communitas [6].

In this work, we present an AR technology used to create augmented "live" wine labels (section II) and to evaluate its impact on consumer experience dimensions, satisfaction, and re-usage intentions towards the application, as well as attitude and purchase intentions towards the wine product (section III). Section IV provides the conclusion of the study.

II. Augmented Reality Design for Live Wine Label

An AR wine label application was developed using Unity 2018.4.31f1 and Vuforia Engine 10.2. The underlying application was implemented for Android mobile devices.

The wine "live" label application is launched to the user mobile device, as follows: users are prompt to target their mobile camera to the front bottle label; once the camera recognizes the target image, the AR application generates the augmented multimedia content which is then shown on the users' smartphone (Figure 1). Specifically, the AR content of the application includes:

- Videos of the winery's production procedures such as harvesting and crushing grapes, fermenting, maturing, and bottling.
- Interactive and 360o videos of the infrastructure of the winery.
- Videos and animation narratives about wine products.
- Information about the wine ingredients and calories in text format and short animated clips.

Figure1. Wine Live Label.

The user can interact with the AR content by selecting the proper action from the application menu and the corresponding information pops up. Furthermore, once the user presses the info button that is located on the bottom right side of the application, a 2D animation character appears on the screen providing additional information in both text and audio form such as wine ingredients, calories, and storage temperature. designations.

III. User Experience and Evaluation of the AR Application

To evaluate the AR application and test the study's objectives, a survey was conducted with a self-administered questionnaire through a convenience sam-pling approach. More specifically, the questionnaires were delivered during the Hotelia exhibition in Thessaloniki, Greece (November 18-20, 2022) that was directed to professionals in the field of hotel equipment, as well as catering and coffee services. Seven university students approached attendees of the exhibition and asked them to participate in the survey. Participants that agreed to take part in the survey, were first shown the application by scanning the label of the wine bottle. Then, they completed the questionnaire. In total, 325 questionnaires were completed, whereas 306 were used in subsequent analysis due to incomplete data. Scales developed regarding user experience and user attitude for the wine. All scales exhibited satisfactory internal reliability (Cronbach's alpha exhibited the 0.70 threshold). Mean Scores (M) of factors that affect respondents experience with the AR wine label application revealed that respondents rated the AR experience as highly educational (M=3.82) and entertaining experience (M=3.68). Flow was experienced in a moderate level by participants (M=3.37) while escapism was experienced to a lesser extent (M=2.80). The AR experience was also able to increase respondents' satisfaction with the application and in turn enable them to form positive attitudes (M=4.06) and purchase intentions (M=3.97) for the wine.

IV. Conclusion

AR wine live label application induced the entertainment and educational dimensions of consumer experience, while feelings of flow and escapism were triggered by the AR application to a lesser extent to respondents. Thus, positive feelings and new knowledge can be generated through wine AR label applications. Results also found the increase of respondents' satisfaction with the application and in turn help them form positive attitudes and purchase intentions for the wine. This indicates that AR may provide new business models in the marketing sector of food and beverages to enhance user experience, develop positive attitude of costumers to the products and increase purchase intentions towards the products. Future work will explore further analysis of AR usage in the food and beverages sector.

Acknowledgment

This work has been co-funded by the European Union and Greek national funds through the operational program competitiveness, entrepreneurship, and innovation, under the call research-create-innovate (project code: T2EDK-03856). All statements of fact, opinion or conclusions contained herein are those of the authors and should not be construed as representing the official views or policies of the sponsors.

References

[1] M. Vrigkas, G. Lappas, A. Kleftodimos and A. Triantafillidou, "Augmented reality for wine industry: Past, Present, and Future", in SHS Web of Conferences, Vol. 102, https://doi.org/10.1051/shsconf/202110204006, 2021.

[2] A. Rejeb, K. Rejeb, and H. Treiblmaier, "How augmented reality impacts retail marketing: A state-of-the-art review from a consumer perspective", Journal of Strategic Marketing DOI: 10.1080/0965254X.2021.1972439, 2021.

[3] S. H. Y. Hsu, H. T., Tsou and J. S. Chen, "Yes, we do. Why not use augmented reality? customer responses to experiential presentations of AR-based applications". Journal of Retailing and Consumer Services, vol. 62, 2021

[4] N. Vaidyanathan and S. Henningsson, "Designing augmented reality services for enhanced customer experiences in retail", Journal of Service Management, Vol. 34, o. 1, pp. 78-99, 2022.

[5] C. Gentile, N. Spiller and G. Noci, "How to sustain the customer experience: An overview of experience components that co-create value with the customer", European Management Journal, vol. 25, no. 5, pp. 395-410, 2007.

[6] A. Triantafillidou and G. Siomkos, "Consumption experience outcomes: satisfaction, nostalgia intensity, word-of-mouth communication and behavioural intentions", Journal of Consumer Marketing, vol. 31, no. 6/7, pp. 526-540, 2014.

CryptoPad: Dedicated Device for Convenient and Secure Wallet

Jione Choi
Hardware Security Laboratory
Korea University
Seoul, South Korea
wldnjs9935@korea.ac.kr

Kiseok Jeon
Hardware Security Laboratory
Korea University
Seoul, South Korea
amt203@korea.ac.kr

Junghee Lee
Hardware Security Laboratory
Korea University
Seoul, South Korea
j_lee@korea.ac.kr

Junsik Sim
Hardware Security Laboratory
Korea University
Seoul, South Korea
jssim@korea.ac.kr

Myungsun Kim
Intelligence Computing Laboratory
Hansung University
Seoul, South Korea
kmsjames@hansung.ac.kr

***Abstract*—As attacks against cryptocurrencies, such as stealing private keys or executing fraudulent transactions to transfer users' assets to attackers' addresses, increase, so does the significance of wallet security. There has always been a trade-off between convenience and security of various types of wallets. In this paper, we present CryptoPad, a dedicated device wallet, to address this issue. CryptoPad is a device where only pre-installed apps can run. CryptoPad is as convenient as a software wallet because a regular software wallet is installed on it. At the same time, we show that it is as secure as a hardware wallet through threat analysis.**

Keywords-Security; Cryptocurrency; Wallet.

I. INTRODUCTION

As the demand for cryptocurrency grows, the importance of cryptocurrency wallets has also increased. A wallet is a device or program that stores a key and allows access to coins. A wallet contains a public key (wallet address) and a private key needed to sign a transaction. Anyone who knows the private key can control the coins associated with the address. Since a wallet is essential in today's cryptocurrency transactions, there are many types of wallets. Levels of security and convenience vary with types of wallets.

North Korean cybercriminals had a banner year in 2021, launching on cryptocurrency platforms where they extracted nearly $400 million worth of digital assets. These attacks targeted primarily at investment firms and centralized exchanges, and made use of phishing lures, code exploits, malware, and advanced social engineering to siphon funds out of these organizations' Internet-connected software wallets into addresses controlled by Democratic People's Republic of Korea (DPRK) [4]. Through these attacks, the importance of wallet's security is further emphasized.

A software wallet implemented in a program or a web browser has the advantage of being simple to use. Thus, it is popular among users who are new to the service. However, the software wallet should be connected to the network, and if its code contains a vulnerability, the private key of the user maybe at a risk. A hardware wallet, on the other hand, is typically not connected to the network but to a software wallet only when necessary; even then, the key never leaves the hardware wallet, which provides strong security.

While the hardware wallet is considered as the most secure wallet as of now, it is not as convenient as a software wallet because it is required to be connected to a software wallet each time a transaction is made. To make a transaction, both hardware and software wallets must be available to the user. Since they are maintained by different organizations, their compatibility is not always guaranteed as they are updated independently. The hardware wallet requires additional intervention of the user to confirm the transaction to be made.

To overcome those shortcomings of the hardware wallet without sacrificing security, we propose a novel concept: a wallet utilizing a dedicated device, named CryptoPad. It is a dedicated device because only pre-installed apps are available, and users are not allowed to install a new app of their choice. The pre-installed apps include a regular software wallet and some other essential apps. A user can make a transaction using a regular software wallet in CryptoPad, which provides the same level of convenience with the software wallet. At the same time, the same level of security with the hardware wallet is offered by the dedicated device equipped with security features such as software installation prevention for thwarting malware installation, behavioral whitelisting for verifying the integrity of the code being executed, and randomization for preventing code reuse attacks. In this paper, we introduce this new concept, and discuss how and why CryptoPad offers strong security comparable to hardware wallets.

The contributions of this paper are summarized as follows.

• A novel concept of a wallet is introduced: a dedicated device for a crypto wallet.

• Threats to wallets and their countermeasures are analyzed.

• Through threat analysis, we show that CryptoPad offers comparable security to a hardware wallet.

II. BACKGROUND

In this section, we examine the software wallet and the hardware wallet, and describe the security components and vulnerabilities of each wallet.

A. *Software Wallet*

A software wallet is literally a wallet written in software. It is connected to the network, which means it is ready to use. Those wallets in central exchanges are always connected to the network, while those running on local devices become online only if necessary. These come in the form of plugins or applications used on a desktop PC, laptop, smartphone, or other digital device where the private and public keys of a user are stored. This wallet is thought to be the most convenient. Users can also utilize software wallets to store different currencies, check transaction history, and set up automatic payments, among other things.

Software wallets provide a variety of security technologies. Most wallets use Secure Hash Algorithm (SHA), Elliptic Curve Digital Signature Algorithm (ECDSA) key generation algorithms as they are built for existing blockchains [12]. The encryption safeguards the wallet from unauthorized access. It also encrypts the private key. Moreover, there are wallets that support multi-signatures or two-factor authentication. In addition, the majority of software wallets allow backup and recovery in the event that the wallet is lost or stolen. Using seed phrases is one of the most popular way to backup and recover the private key [7].

Despite these security features, software wallets are susceptible to a variety of attacks. The objective of the attack is to steal the private key stored in the wallet. The attacker may employ a phishing attack [3] to obtain a user's private key or other sensitive information from the software wallet. Through phishing attacks, it is possible for an attacker to install malware. When malware is installed, the attacker can take control of the wallet and may steal the private key. It can also be achieved by vulnerabilities in the software wallets or other applications in the same device. By exploiting vulnerabilities, the attacker may inject a malicious code, or reuse existing code maliciously. Without installation of malware, the attacker can still compromise the wallet.

B. *Hardware Wallet*

A hardware wallet, is a physical device for storing keys. It is regarded as the safest option to store digital assets because it is not connected to the Internet and thus less susceptible to hacking and other security breaches.

Even while a transaction is being made, the hardware wallet protects the private key by keeping the key to itself. It does not provide any software interface to read the key. To make a transaction, the software wallet sends a transaction to the hardware wallet. Then the hardware wallet generates a signature with the private key and returns the signature only. Thus, the private key never leaves the hardware wallet.

Even though it is not possible to read the private key, there still exists a way to make a transaction that is not intended by the user. The software wallet could be compromised where a malicious code is injected. The transaction from the software wallet may be different from the transaction made by the user. To prevent a fraud transaction, the hardware wallet requires additional intervention of the user. The user needs to check and confirm every transaction. However, not all the hardware wallets show the entire transaction including destination address. Some wallets only verifies whether the user wants to make a transaction or not. Some other wallets show the transaction to be checked, but it is the user's responsibility to validate the correctness of the transaction. The validation cannot be automated. Even if a user realizes coins are sent to a wrong address later, it is usually too late because most cryptocurrencies do not support revocation.

III. CRYPTOPAD

We introduce CryptoPad, a a dedicated device for a crypto wallet, where only pre-installed apps can run. We named it as CryptoPad because we prototyped it on a tablet modifying Android, but it is not restricted to a tablet.

CryptoPad is as convenient as a software wallet because a regular software wallet is running on it. It does not require the user for additional connection and manual intervention. It provides the same user experience with a software wallet. CryptoPad offers strong security comparable to a hardware wallet with additional security elements, which are explained in the following subsections.

A. *No Installation*

CryptoPad does not allow installation of any app by the user. Only pre-installed apps are available. If any update or installation of an app is required, the whole CryptoPad disk image, including the Operating System (OS), is updated after verification of its integrity.

It may cause a little inconvenience to the user. However, most crypto services, such as exchanges, Decentralized Finance (DeFi), and Non-Fungible Token (NFT) trading, provide a web interface. Thus, there is no problem for the user to access those services with the pre-installed web browser. This is one of the reasons why we prototyped CryptoPad on a tablet, which provides a large screen.

Though users cannot install individual apps by themselves, they can choose a package of apps which are included in an OS image. We provide multiple OS images, each of which includes different packages of apps. For example, OS image A includes MetaMask only, while OS image B includes MetaMask and Opera Crypto Browser, and OS image C may include MetaMask, Opera, and FireFox. Users can choose one of images A, B, and C depending on their purpose and interest. When an image is chosen, the whole firmware of CryptoPad is updated to the chose image in the same way as Android is updated.

By prohibiting installation, CryptoPad prevents installation of malicious apps. To steal the private key or make a fraud transaction, adversaries need to execute at least a small piece of a malicious code. It is impossible for adversaries to install a malicious app because CryptoPad does not have any mechanism for it. It is especially useful to prevent phishing and smishing, where victims are deceived by fake links that lead to installation of malicious apps.

B. Behavioral Whitelisting

Whitelisting verifies the integrity of pre-installed apps. It compares the hash of their code with the reference integrity metric when they launch and while they are running. If the hash mismatches, the app is blocked.

The whitelisting allows only known normal behavior while the blacklisting prohibits known malicious behavior. The blacklisting is the technique employed by malware scanners. Since only pre-installed apps are allowed to run on the CryptoPad, the whitelisting technique can be implemented in an efficient and effective manner. The whitelisting offers stronger security than blacklisting because the latter can prevent known malware only, while the former can thwart unknown malware as well.

The whitelisting can be used to defend against code injection attacks. Even though installation of malware is prohibited, adversaries may inject a malicious code by exploiting vulnerabilities of pre-installed apps. If any code is executed, which is not a part of genuine pre-installed apps, it is immediately blocked.

C. Address Space Layout Randomization (ASLR)

Address Space Layout Randomization (ASLR) is a technique to thwart exploits which rely on knowing the location of the target code or data. ASLR randomizes the location of key memory areas within an address space to make it probabilistically hard for an attacker to gain control over aprocess [6]. ASLR helps defend against code reuse attacks, such as return oriented programming attacks.

CryptoPad is prototyped by modifying the Android Open Source Project (AOSP). Since Android 4.0 introduced ASLR, library load ordering randomization was accepted into the AOSP in 2015, and was included from the Android 7.0 release [11]. The current version of ASOP supports ASLR. Therefore, CryptoPad can utilize the ASLR security function.

IV. ATTACK SCENARIOS

We analyze attack scenarios to wallets and show that CryptoPad offers comparable security to a hardware wallet. Since CryptoPad and a hardware wallet have different defense mechanisms, an apple-to-apple comparison cannot be made, but through threat analysis, we discuss how CryptoPad and a hardware wallet defend against attack scenarios.

CryptoPad and a hardware wallet are different in preventing attacks while transactions are made. After analyzing attacks scenarios in subsection IV-A, we discuss how CryptoPad and a hardware wallet mitigate them in subsection IV-B. There are common issues and defense mechanisms in CryptoPad and a hardware wallet. They are discussed in subsection IV-C.

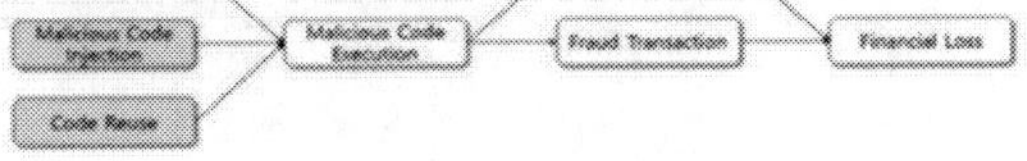

Figure 1. Attack scenarios to wallets.

A. Threat Analysis

The attack scenarios are depicted in Figure 1. Attack scenarios to blockchain protocols and smart contracts are not included because they are not directly related with wallets.

The goal of the adversaries is to steal assets. It can be achieved by stealing the private key or counterfeiting a transaction. If a wallet is physically stolen, adversaries may extract the private key by physical access. The private key can also be stolen by a malicious code. Adversaries may gain control and run a malicious code to extract the private key. If they can run a malicious code, it is also possible to make fraud transactions. A malicious code can be executed by installation, code injection and code reuse.

Malware can be installed in a variety of ways, such as phishing or exploiting vulnerabilities. Wallet's malware is malicious software that is specifically designed to target wallets and the cryptocurrency stored in them. For example, Microsoft is currently warning against Cryware, which targets software wallets. It collects and exfiltrates data directly from non-custodial cryptocurrency wallets, also known as software wallets. Because software wallets are executed locally on a device and provide easier access to cryptographic keys needed to make transactions, more and more threats are targeting them [9].

Wallet's code injection attack is a type of attack where a malicious code is inserted into the wallet to gain access to private keys and other information. In 2019, a code injection attack was discovered that allowed malicious actors to inject a malicious code into the BitPay app, potentially giving them access to users' private data [1]. It was injected through a third party NodeJS package used by the BitPay apps, which had been modified to load a malicious code.

Code reuse attacks are software exploits in which an attacker directs control flow through existing codes on a malicious purpose [2]. For example, return-oriented programming manipulates the return address stored in the stack so that the behavior of the software may be changed for the purpose of adversaries.

B. Defense Mechanisms

A malicious code cannot be executed in a hardware wallet because it does not provide any interface to install or run an arbitrary code. However, some hardware wallets support firmware update. If the update procedure has a vulnerability, a malicious code could sneak into the wallet.

Adversaries may penetrate to the software wallet connected to the hardware wallet instead of directly attacking the hardware wallet. They may execute a malicious code in the software wallet, or another app running on the same device. Even if they are compromised, the private key in the hardware wallet cannot be exposed because the hardware wallet does not allow it. However, the compromised software wallet may make a fraud transaction that is not intended by the user. It is user's responsibility to validate the transaction signed by the hardware wallet.

CryptoPad prevents execution of a malicious code by the security features presented in Section III, whereas a hardware wallet prevents stealing keys by a hardware mechanism even if a malicious code is executed in the connected software wallet. Though the defense mechanisms are different, we expect that CryptoPad offers comparable security because it is dedicated only to pre-installed apps, which makes it efficient and effective to employ strong security techniques.

C. Common Issues

When assets are at rest in wallets, CryptoPad offers the exact same level of security with hardware wallets. If CryptoPad is turned off or disconnected from the network, it works identically as hardware wallets. There is no way for adversaries to read the private key or to make a fraud transaction through software-based attacks while CryptoPad and a hardware wallet are not connected to anywhere.

Most (if not all) hardware wallets, however, do not have defense mechanisms against physical attacks. Adversaries may access the private key by cracking the user authentication method such as a password or Personal Identification Number (PIN). Furthermore, if the wallet is physically accessible, adversaries can depackage chips in the wallet and read internal signals by micro-probing. If CryptoPad or a hardware wallet is physically stolen, the private key stored there is at a risk.

V. Discussion

Defense mechanisms cannot be perfect in CryptoPad as well as hardware wallets. In this section, we discuss security issues of the defense mechanisms in CryptoPad.

The most crucial aspect of the behavioral whitelisting is building and maintaining a database of trusted applications [10]. This can be viewed as a question on how to trust the initial pre-installed applications. For CryptoPad, we consider this out of scope, because we only install apps that have been verified by other means such as Google Play Protect. Since CryptoPad allows only a small number of apps, only publicly well-known apps are pre-installed.

If the database is tampered, a malicious code may not be filtered. For CryptoPad, the database is generated while the OS image is being built, and the database is deployed with the OS image. Once deployed, CryptoPad never updates the database. It does not need any capability of updating the database. Thus, to tamper the database, a malicious code, which updates the database, must be installed or injected first. It introduces a deadlock condition where adversaries need a malicious code in order to execute a malicious code.

If adversaries manage to execute a malicious code by reusing existing gadgets, however, the whitelisting could be circumvented. By randomly setting the offset, ASLR makes it harder for adversaries to locate the address of target gadgets. As moved to a 64-bit system, full-ASLR [8] and Position Independent Executable (PIE) were implemented, enhancing the effectiveness of ASLR.

There are still ways to bypass ASLR. For example, ASLR can be bypassed via the Branch Target Buffer (BTB) [5]. An exploit can cause an attacker to establish a BTB conflict between the branch command of the attacker process and the user-level kernel running the victim process. These collisions modify the timing of the attacker's code, enabling the attacker to identify known branch instructions in the address space of the target process or kernel. Even if the base address is random, the target address can be computed in this scenario. However, most attacks on ASLR are based on side-channel analysis, which requires the attacker to run a process fully controlled by the attacker. It is feasible for general-purpose devices, but not for CryptoPad because it is another deadlock situation for adversaries.

VI. Conclusions

In this paper, we introduced CryptoPad, a dedicated device for a crypto wallet. We discussed how the security features of CryptoPad thwart execution of a malicious code, offering comparable security to a hardware wallet. Since a user can use a regular wallet on CryptoPad, it offers as convenient user experience as a software wallet. For interested readers, more information is available at our website [13].

References

[1] Bitpay, How bitpay is securing the copay and bitpay wallets. Available online: https://bitpay.com/blog/copay-npm-security-update/ [retrieved: Mar, 2023]

[2] T. Bletsch, "Code-reuse attacks: New frontiers and defenses," Ph.D.dissertation, 2011, aAI3463747.

[3] M. Bosamia and D. Patel, "Wallet payments recent potential threats andvulnerabilities with its possible security measures," International Journalof Computer Sciences and Engineering, vol. 7, pp. 810–817, 01 2019.

[4] Chainalysis. North korean hackers have prolific year as theirunlaundered cryptocurrency holdings reach all-time high. Available online: https://blog.chainalysis.com/reports/north-korean-hackers-have-prolific-year-as-their-total-unlaundered-cryptocurrency-holdings-reach-all-time-high/ [retrieved: Mar, 2023]

[5] D. Evtyushkin, D. Ponomarev, and N. Abu-Ghazaleh, "Jump overaslr: Attacking branch predictors to bypass aslr," in 2016 49th AnnualIEEE/ACM International Symposium on Microarchitecture (MICRO),2016, pp. 1–13.

[6] S. Liebergeld and M. Lange, "Android security, pitfalls and lessonslearned," in Information Sciences and Systems 2013. Springer, 2013,pp. 409–417.

[7] Y. Liu, R. Li, X. Liu, J. Wang, L. Zhang, C. Tang, and H. Kang,"An efficient method to enhance bitcoin wallet security," in 2017 11thIEEE International Conference on Anti-counterfeiting, Security, andIdentification (ASID), 2017, pp. 26–29.

[8] H. Marco-Gisbert and I. Ripoll, "On the effectiveness of full-aslr on 64-bit linux," in Proceedings of the In-Depth Security Conference, 2014.

[9] Microsoft. (2022) In hot pursuit of 'cryware': Defending hot wallets from attacks. Available online: https://www.microsoft.com/en-us/security/blog/2022/05/17/in-hot-pursuit-of-cryware-defending-hot-wallets-from-attacks/ [retrieved: Mar, 2023]

[10] H. Pareek, S. Romana, and P. Eswari, "Application whitelisting: approaches and challenges," International Journal of Computer Science,Engineering and Information Technology (IJCSEIT), vol. 2, no. 5, pp.13–18, 2012.

[11] V. Parikh and P. Mateti, "Aslr and rop attack mitigations for arm-basedandroid devices," 11 2017, pp. 350–363.

[12] S. Suratkar, M. Shirole, and S. Bhirud, "Cryptocurrency wallet: Areview," in 2020 4th International Conference on Computer, Communication and Signal Processing (ICCCSP), 2020, pp. 1–7.

[13] CryptoPad. (2023) "CryptoPad Website" http://www.cryptopad.io/ [retrieved: April 2023]

The Aggregator as a Trust Builder in a Renewable Energy System

Lasse Berntzen
School of Business
University of South-Eastern Norway
Horten, Norway
e-mail: lasse.berntzen@usn.no

Marius Rohde Johannessen
School of Business
University of South-Eastern Norway
Horten, Norway
e-mail: marius.johannessen@usn.no

Qian Meng
School of Business
University of South-Eastern Norway
Horten, Norway
e-mail: qian.meng@usn.no

Abstract—**This paper focuses on the role of the aggregator as a trust builder in a smart grid with consumers and prosumers. An aggregator plays a new role in the energy market and represents a group of consumers and prosumers toward the market. The aggregator can negotiate prices and trade flexibility for its consumers and prosumers. Trading flexibility is vital to shave peaks in energy consumption. A survey among early adopters of renewable energy in households revealed a lack of trust in transferring control of electric vehicle charging, heating, and household appliances to an aggregator. The paper proposes measures to improve trust in the energy market, focusing on the aggregator role. Three categories of measures are suggested: regulatory, technical, and organizational, combined with a plain language policy.**

Keywords-smart grid; flexibility; trust; prosumer; aggregator; ecosystem; plain language.

I. INTRODUCTION

A prosumer is both a producer and a consumer. In the electricity market, a prosumer produces electric energy from renewable sources, such as solar panels. Excess energy can be sold to the grid. An aggregator plays a new role in the energy market and represents a group of consumers and prosumers toward the market. The aggregator can negotiate prices and trade flexibility for its consumers and prosumers.

A recent survey by the authors among early adopters of smart home technologies and renewable energy production in households relieved a significant lack of trust in the energy market [1]. Trust has decreased even more as energy costs have soared throughout 2022. In Norway, the Facebook group demanding lower electricity prices has 620.000 members, and the media presents new stories about the consequences of soaring prices every day. Polls show that government support is at an all-time low, and commentators go a long way in pointing to the energy crisis as a reason for this lack of support. It seems that trust is at an all-time low, at least where energy is concerned, yet trust is perhaps the most critical factor for conducting effective transactions and making things happen smoothly. A low level of trust in government and institutions increases the risk of direct action by citizens [2]. It is even said that trust is the key to understanding the dynamics of social relations, to the extent that it is often viewed as the glue that holds society together [3].

The current energy crisis emphasizes the consequences of falling trust levels. The electricity market seems to be part of the problem since pricing mechanisms are complex and challenging to understand for the average citizen. For example, the algorithm "Euphemia" predicts future prices and is complicated and hard to explain. The whitepaper describing the algorithm's work is 53 pages long and very technical [4]. This complexity is likely part of why people distrust the energy market. When market experts talk to the media and try to explain why prices are high, explanations tend to vary between different factors, such as hydro basin water levels, the cost of natural gas or CO_2, and this leads to confused public thinking that the real reason simply is that "someone" wants prices to remain high.

Based on the above, it seems that communication, or rather a lack of clear communication, is part of the problem. We know from other fields, such as health, that plain and understandable communication is essential for trust [5].

In this paper, we propose three classes of measures: regulatory, technical, and organizational, combined with a plain language policy to alleviate the current situation and contribute to a higher level of trust in energy market institutions, which can aid the transition towards green energy. The measures are shown in Fig. 1.

Fig. 2 illustrates how traditional power grids transfer electricity from producers to consumers. The generated electricity by the power plants goes through the transmission network operated by the Transmission System Operator (TSO) and the regional network operated by the Distribution System Operator (DSO), then to the end user. The transfer is one-way; the end user must pay for electricity based on a tariff.

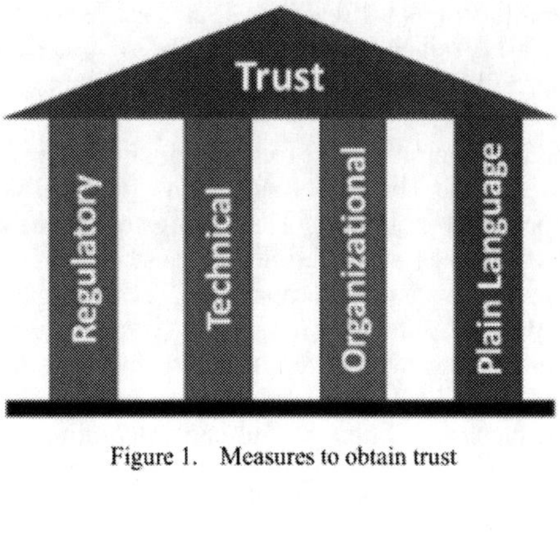

Figure 1. Measures to obtain trust

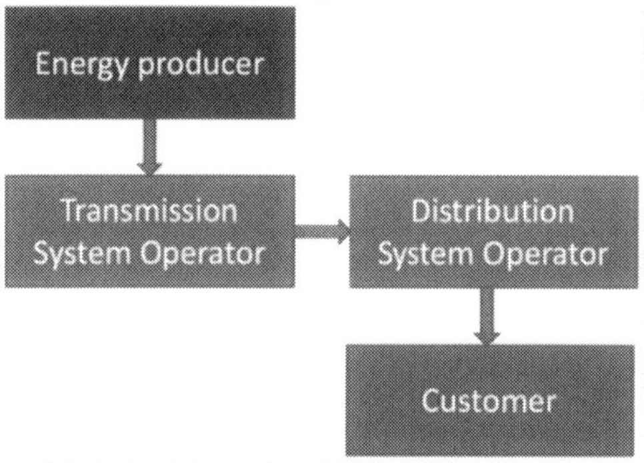

Figure 2. Traditional power grid.

With the development of renewable energy sources, consumers can produce electricity from solar panels, windmills, and geothermal power. This new role is often called prosumer. Smart grids enable a two-way energy transfer, allowing prosumers to produce and sell energy. A smart meter records the amount of energy transferred in the power ecosystem.

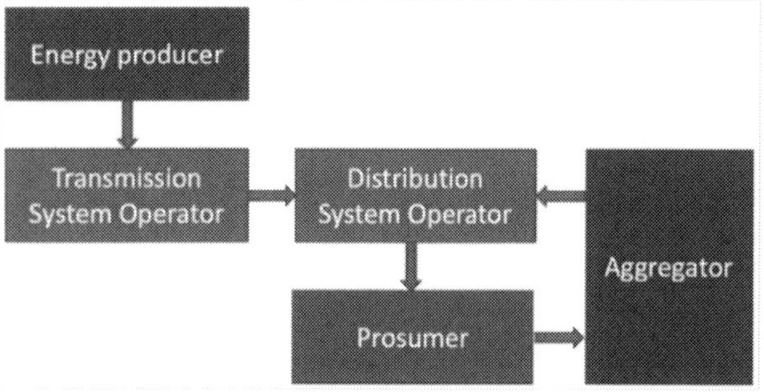

Figure 3. Power grid with prosumers and aggregators.

The aggregator is a separate entity representing several prosumers. An independent aggregator is defined in the EU Clean Energy Package (CEP) in Art. 2 (19) of the Directive (EU) 2019/944 [6] as "a market participant engaged in aggregation who is not affiliated to the customer's supplier." Aggregation is "a function performed by a natural or legal person who combines multiple customer loads or generated electricity for sale, purchase or auction in any electricity market." The traditional suppliers can provide aggregator services like demand response, but they haven't taken this responsibility since their main business is selling energy. Therefore, the role of independent aggregators has emerged [7][8].

The aggregator may negotiate terms with consumers and prosumers and handle transactions internally between consumers and prosumers. The aggregator may also provide electricity storage and offer electricity storage as a service to customers without storage capability. The aggregator plays an essential role in achieving flexibility. Grid flexibility refers to the ability of a power system to maintain a balance between generation and load during uncertainty, resulting in increased grid efficiency, resiliency, and the integration of variable renewables into the grid [9]. The gain from such flexibility is savings for the prosumer since electricity is cheaper in off-peak periods. Flexibility can postpone infrastructure upgrades and investments due to better grid utilization for the TSO and the DSO.

The authors were part of the ERA-NET+ Smart-MLA project [10] that designed and developed a cloud-based aggregator solution to optimize demand response and increase grid flexibility for renewable energy usage. Smart-MLA aimed to raise consumer and community awareness of demand response aggregating mechanisms. The project created user-friendly interfaces accessible through web pages and web services, allowing consumers to configure, control and monitor their appliances. Aggregators could also access these web services to securely analyze, plan, and forecast energy consumption and generation without the need for own infrastructure.

In the summer of 2021, the authors surveyed early adopters of home automation technology as part of the Smart-MLA project. The respondents were approached using Norwegian Facebook groups relevant to smart homes. The survey asked about demographic information, existing household installations, and the sentiments towards transferring control of electric vehicle charging, heating, and household appliances to an aggregator. The survey was open for five days and attracted 209 respondents. Fifty-two respondents used the opportunity to answer open-ended questions [1].

One clear result was a lack of trust in the energy market and its actors. Generally, the respondents expressed a low willingness to hand over control unless highly compensated. A large majority were positive about flexibility but wanted to remain in control.

One response was: "*Energy companies will never be allowed to control anything in my house. With their hidden terms and conditions, they have repeatedly shown that they can't be trusted.*"

Another was: "*The DSOs...have neglected to invest in the grid for the past 25 years while paying out hundreds of millions to shareholders. It's time they step up without shoving the [financial] burden onto consumers.*"

And a third was: "*I don't trust them. What if something goes wrong?... and if the system is able to cut costs, that won't get back to consumers.*"

These are three representative responses from the survey. There may be many reasons for the lack of trust, but the most important is a long-lasting competition with incomprehensible and incomparable terms.

The results from the survey were the inspiration to investigate possible ways for aggregators to build trust with consumers and prosumers.

The rest of the paper is organized as follows: Section II discusses flexibility and trust, followed by Section III, proposing measures for prosumers to trust an aggregator. Section IV concludes the paper.

II. Flexibility and Trust

The electricity demand varies throughout the day. The price of electricity follows the demand. Shifting some of the load to periods with less demand is advantageous for all parties. The consumers will reduce their electricity bills, while the grid operator can delay investments in new grid infrastructure.

Flexibility happens when consumers and prosumers offer to shift their loads. A single household will not contribute much, but if hundreds or thousands of consumers and prosumers provide flexibility, the impact will be high. The peaks will be shaved by shifting some load to periods with less demand.

A flexible consumer or prosumer can decide to postpone consumption of energy, e.g., for electric car charging or heating, until the total demand for energy becomes lower. The distribution system operator or an aggregator can handle flexibility. A typical example of flexibility is to render control of electric car charging, with the constraint that the car should be fully charged at 7 am in the morning.

Flexibility depends on trust. A consumer or prosumer must trust that the aggregator or distribution system operator fulfills their obligations, e.g., that the car is fully charged at 7 am. A consumer or prosumer that lacks trust will not transfer control to a not trustworthy entity.

In the energy market, the aggregators, prosumers, and other actors must deal with the complexity of interacting with organizations and thus face the necessity to reduce this complexity before participating. According to the complexity reduction mechanism suggested by Luhmann [11], familiarity and trust address essential aspects of the complexity within organizations. Familiarity and information sharing inside organizations and crossing the organizations are fundamental for building trust.

Piderit and Flowerday [12] observe two different views of trust: The first is based on confidence or risk in the predictability of the other party's actions, and in this instance, parties hedge themselves against uncertain events through guarantees, insurance, or law. The second view is based on confidence in the other party's goodwill, which relies on faith in the other party's integrity.

The first view relies on regulations, while the second relies on the parties' relationship.

During the work for the project SMART-MLA, the aggregators will plan and forecast the consumption and generation from the customers and prosumers (wind power, solar power) in a community. The aggregators and prosumers trust each other in the common concern for climate change, interest in new technologies, and environmental contribution. In contrast, the prosumers don't trust the aggregators for the issues of security of energy supply, immature technologies and business models, and expensive investments. The challenge is more prominent for renewable energy sources since photovoltaic and wind power must be produced instantly when sunshine or wind is present. The energy created from the sun and wind varies with weather conditions and is hence more challenging to integrate [13]. Therefore, strengthening the trust between the prosumers and the aggregators becomes a significant issue.

III. MEASURES TO CREATE TRUST

As we have demonstrated above, there is a strong link between grid flexibility and trust among aggregators, consumers, and prosumers. We propose to make efforts within the four categories below to build trust for the actors and reduce the risk of misbehavior: Regulatory measures, technical measures, and organizational transformations combined with a plain language policy.

A. Regulatory Frameworks

Without trusting others in the electric energy market, people would be confronted with the incomprehensible complexity of considering every possible eventuality of every person around before deciding what to do. Such complexity would be so overwhelming that, in many cases, people would refrain from acting. Trust is not the only complexity reduction method; rules are powerful techniques for reducing complexity. However, even when there are rules, trust is essential because there is no guarantee that other people will fully abide by them [14].

Therefore, regulatory measures are one of the pillars of building trust so that participants behave within a specific framework and non-compliance can be punished. Parliamentary acts, government regulations, and the energy sector, through self-regulation, may establish regulatory measures. Regulatory measures, such as EU and Norwegian national regulations, may instruct the market actors to comply with rules and regulations.

1) EU Energy Regulations

According to the EU Clean Energy Package (CEP), Member States shall enable demand response through independent aggregation. Directive (EU) 2019/944 Art. 17 contains the principles the national regulatory frameworks must respect [6]. Regulation (EU) 2019/943 Art. 59 1(e) states that a new network code can be developed in the area of demand response, including rules on aggregation, energy storage, and demand curtailment rules [15]. Network codes are typically used to harmonize the regulatory frameworks at the national level [16].

Under European frameworks, the energy participants have confidence in their clear expectations of what other actors will do, based on EU regulations and previous interactions.

The regulations reduce the need for extensive negotiations, detail resolution, tight transaction control, etc. These EU regulations aim at long-term orientation, then increase the acceptance of interdependence and create commitment among energy actors. Furthermore, trust built on the common EU energy frameworks also reduces risk and transaction costs since these frameworks are essential in almost every contractual agreement. Therefore, EU energy regulations enable trust among the participants as well as the quality of business relationships. Without EU energy regulations, the lack of trust creates control-oriented and defensive communication that degrades communication and then cuts off the energy transaction across the countries.

2) Norwegian National Regulations

The Norwegian electrical energy market opened for competition when the Energy Act entered into force in 1991 [17]. The Norwegian Energy Regulatory Authority (NVE-RME) ensures the regulatory activities. NVE-RME has played an active role as an energy market regulator in developing network regulation besides EU regulations, real market access for all customers, simplified supplier switching procedures, securing security and quality of supply, and efficient regulation of the energy system operation in Norway. In 2018, NVE suggested a mandatory structure for the grid tariff to incentivize lower peak loads [18].

For the prosumers and other participants in the power market, official regulations can standardize contract terms, establish a common tariff structure, promote competition, and make it easier for customers to change electric power suppliers and connected services. According to the Norwegian official regulator NVE, all consumers have a right to produce and sell surplus electricity. The network companies are obliged to connect prosumers and receive their production. Prosumers feeding in less than 100 kW are not charged the fixed component for generation. Prosumers can choose their own electricity supplier that supplies their need for electricity and buy surplus electricity from the prosumer. In 2020 there were about 6 800 prosumers in Norway [19].

3) Self-regulation

The energy sector can take responsibility through self-regulation. In 2020, Renewables Norway [20] and Distriktsenergi established "Safe Energy Trading" to make the industry more transparent and customer friendly. The certification scheme allows energy companies to prove they follow best practices and commit themselves to improve customer relations. Self-regulation is a market-driven approach to tackle industry challenges and implement regulations by adjusting marketing and enhancing customer dialogue in line with requirements.

B. Technical Measures

Albinson, Balaji, and Chu [21] argue that technology can help build trust among stakeholders and create benefits for society. They suggest four pillars of trust, shown in Table I.

Their use of technology focuses on information handling. In the energy market context, two specific technologies may be particularly relevant: (1) Advanced Metering Systems (AMS) to give consumers and prosumers more insight into electricity use and production, and (2) Blockchain technology, sometimes referred to as Distributed Ledger Technology (DLT), which makes energy transactions unalterable and transparent through decentralization and cryptographic hashing.

1) Advanced Metering System (AMS)

For customers in the distribution grid, AMS with smart meters can offer the technology for new grid tariffs based on hourly metering consumption, which will incentivize the flexibility of consumers and prosumers.

TABLE I. FOUR PILLARS OF TRUST [21]

Transparency and accessibility
• Enabling customers to easily evaluate the company and its offerings. • Making business terms, such as additional fees, privacy policies, and terms of service readily accessible and easily understandable. • Clarifying how self-learning algorithms operate. • Providing line of sight into supply chains.
Ethics and responsibility
• Ironing out complaints in a sensitive and timely manner. • Stopping misinformation in its tracks. • Encouraging inclusion with tools that test fairness and detect biases. • Implementing safeguards to promote stakeholder welfare along with digital controls that prevent unethical or inappropriate use of technology.
Privacy and control
• Putting control of personal data in users' hands. • Improving accuracy of consumer data. • Being frugal with personally identifiable information.
Security and reliability
• Verifying the identity of people claiming to be customers or providers to reduce impersonation and fraud. • Using automation and AI to reduce errors and fraud. • Proactively alerting users in the event of suspicious account activity.

According to the Norwegian regulations, the smart meters should have standardized interfaces that allow for communication with external equipment; be able to connect different types of meters (e.g., gas, heat, water); secure data storage in cases of voltage outage; send and receive price information (from energy contracts and network tariffs) and signals for load control and earth fault detection [22].

The smart meters are designed to meter the power flow in both directions, to and from the customer, enabling customers to invest in renewable energy sources to become prosumers.

2) Blockchain Technology

Transparency and accountability are essential for building trust. A blockchain allows the actors to store transaction data in an immutable, distributed ledger. Smart contracts that can be executed on the blockchain can replace intermediaries in the transaction process [23].

The Smart-MLA project developed a blockchain-based solution for handling settlements between an aggregator and its prosumers [24]. A private blockchain was chosen since the costs of registering a transaction on the blockchain was many times higher than the actual amount of the transaction.

Smart contracts on the blockchain are self-executing when agreed conditions are met. It is possible to use smart contracts to set constraints on selling and buying prices.

C. *Organizational Transformations*

Ahmad and Huvila studied the relationship between organizational change and information sharing. They found that if organizational changes are perceived positively, trust between employees and in management will increase, which consequently will enhance information sharing [25]. We believe that trust between prosumers and aggregators will also increase if the organizational changes are perceived positively. More information sharing means more transparency.

Trust can be seen as a cornerstone of work relationships and a key component of organizational effectiveness between the prosumers and aggregators. The "cooperative" model can be the organizational measure for the aggregator to build trust [26].

The International Cooperative Alliance (ICA) defines the term "cooperative" as "an autonomous association of persons united voluntarily to meet their common economic, social, and cultural needs and aspirations through jointly owned and democratically controlled enterprise" [27].

ICA has set out the collaboration principles: self-help, self-responsibility, democracy, equality, equity, and solidarity [27]. The company and the partner must also reflect four ethical values: honesty, openness, social responsibility, and caring for others. In addition, both parties need to be communication-based, multilevel, culturally rooted, and dynamic. In the smart grid ecosystem, the aggregators and prosumers must reflect these cooperative values when they want to build trust in each other [28]. Trust and sharing information will enhance each other's commitment and motivation to achieve grid flexibility.

D. *Plain Language*

Plain language initiatives emerged from the public sector's need to communicate better with citizens. Studies of public services found that many services and communications from the government were difficult for citizens to understand [29]. Language can be an instrument of inclusion but can also exclude, discriminate, and reinforce existing and unwanted power structures [30]. Plain language initiatives have sprung up to address this in several countries. Plain language is defined as "correct, clear and user-centered language in texts from government" [31]. It involves helping readers understand the text through the organization and structure, breaking up of complex information, simple language, and clear definitions of technical terms.

As there is a clear connection between language, understanding and trust [5], we argue that using plain language is essential for the other three measures to have an effect. There are several approaches to developing plain language, and a plain language strategy should probably involve several of these. One example is readability indexes, algorithms that measure the readability of texts through word recognition, string lengths, etc. [32]. In addition, those responsible for communication with customers' need training in plain language writing techniques, such as guidelines for structuring text, and which words to choose for a given audience.

There are several case studies on the effect of plain language, some of which are presented in [33], showing how different actors in the public sector have worked systematically and strategically to implement plain language in their communication with the outside world. These measures have led to fewer complaints and more satisfied service users simply because they understand the communication they receive. Given the confusion related to electricity pricing mentioned in the introduction, we argue that a plain language strategy from the actors in the energy market can be an essential factor in increasing trust.

Further, in addition to the language in the form of words, visualization could also help explain complex issues and ideas in a business context [34]. Thus, we would also argue for using data-driven dashboards and visualizations to help users understand their energy bills and how prices are set.

IV. Conclusions

This paper focuses on the lack of trust among consumers and prosumers in the energy market. The aggregator/prosumer model presented in Fig. 3 can become essential to the transition to renewable energy. Flexibility can help balance the grid and flatten demand curves at peak hours. Trust is crucial for implementing flexibility, where an aggregator can take control over household consumption.

A survey among early adopters of smart home technology shows that actors will meet strong barriers when getting consumers and prosumers on board. The lack of trust has been present since the deregulation of the Norwegian power market in 1971. The common opinion is that energy actors are more interested in earning money than creating the best situation for consumers and prosumers. Several measures need to be put in place to gain the trust of consumers and prosumers. We point to four essential pillars of trust: regulatory measures, technical measures, and organizational transformations combined with adopting a plain language policy. These measures may help build the necessary trust to make flexibility work.

Acknowledgment

This work was supported by the Manu Net scheme Grant number MNET20/NMCS-3779 and funded through the Research Council of Norway Grant number 322500 with the project title "Cloud-based analysis and diagnosis platform for photovoltaic (PV) prosumers."

References

[1] M. R. Johannessen, L. Berntzen, Q. Meng, B. Vesin, T. Brekke, and I. Laur, "User Sentiments Towards Smart Grid Flexibility - A survey of early adopters' attitude towards allowing third parties to control electricity use in households" 14th International Conference on Advances in Human-oriented and Personalized Mechanisms, Technologies and Services (CENTRIC), IARIA, pp. 41-46, 2021.

[2] M. Kaase, "Interpersonal trust, political trust and non-institutionalised political participation in Western Europe," West European Politics, vol. 22(3), pp. 1–21, 1999.

[3] O. Schilke, M. Reimann, and K. S. Cook, "Trust in Social Relations," Annual Review of Sociology, vol. 47, pp. 239-259, 2021.

[4] Nordpool Group. *Euphemia public description. Single price coupling algorithm.* [Online] Available from: https://www.nordpoolgroup.com/globalassets/download-center/single-day-ahead-coupling/euphemia-public-description.pdf 2023.03.01

[5] P. A. Paprica, K. McGrail, and M. J. Schull, *Plain language about health data is essential for transparency and trust.* The Conversation. October 10th 2019 [Online]. Available from: https://theconversation.com/plain-language-about-health-data-is-essential-for-transparency-and-trust-123319, 2023.03.01.

[6] European Commission. *Directive (EU) 2019/944 of the European Parliament and of the Council of 5 June 2019 on common rules for the internal market for electricity and amending directive 2012/27/EU.* [Online]. Available from: http://data.europa.eu/eli/dir/2019/944 2023.03.01.

[7] R. Bray and B. Woodman, "Barriers to independent aggregators in Europe," EPG Working Paper 1901, 2019.

[8] S. Burger, J.P. Chaves-ávila, C. Batlle, and I. Pérez-Arriaga, "The Value of Aggregators in Electricity Systems," Renewable Sustainable Energy Review, vol. 77, pp. 395–405, 2017.

[9] Cleantech Group. *Smart Grid Flexibility Markets – Entering an Era of Localization.* April 14th, 2020. [Online]. Available from: https://www.cleantech.com/smart-grid-flexibility-markets-entering-an-era-of-localization/ 2023.03.01.

[10] Smart-MLA Consortium. *Project fact sheet.* [Online]. Available from: http://smart-mla.stimasoft.com/wp-content/uploads/2020/02/ERANetSES_SMART_MLA.docx 2023.03.01

[11] N. Luhman, Trust and Power, Wiley, 2017.

[12] R. Piderit and S. Flowerday, "The risk relationship between trust and information sharing in automotive supply chains," World Congress on Internet Security (WorldCIS 2014), IEEE, pp. 80-85, 2014

[13] C. Skar, S. Jaehnert, A. Tomasgard, K.T. Midthun, and M. Fodstad, "Norway's role as a flexibility provider in a renewable Europe", Centre for Sustainable Energy Studies (CenSES), 2013.

[14] F. Fukuyama, Trust: the social virtues and the creation of prosperity. New York: The Free Press, 1995.

[15] European Commission. *Regulation (EU) 2019/943 of the European Parliament and of the Council of 5 June 2019 on the internal market for electricity.* [Online]. Available from: http://data.europa.eu/eli/reg/2019/943 2023.03.01

[16] T. Schittekatte, V. Deschamps, and L. Meeus, "The regulatory framework for independent aggregators", EUI Working Paper RSC 2021/53, the European University Institute, May 2021

[17] Norwegian Ministry of Petroleum and Energy. *Act no. 50 of 29 June 1990: Act relating to the generation, conversion, transmission, trading, distribution and use of energy etc. (The Energy Act).* [Online]. Available from: https://www.climate-laws.org/geographies/norway/laws/the-energy-act-no-50-of-1990 2023.03.01.

[18] NVE. *Høring - forslag til endringer i forskrift om kontroll av nettvirksomhet – tariffer 2018.* (Hearing – proposal for changes in regulations on control of network activities – tariffs 2018) [Online]. Available from: https://www.nve.no/om-nve/regelverk/forskriftsendringer-pa-horing/horingforslag-til-endringer-i-forskrift-om-kontroll-av-nettvirksomhet-tariffer-avsluttet/ 2023.03.01

[19] T. Langset and H. H. Nielsen. *RME Rapport Nr. 6/2021 – National Report 2021. Norwegian Energy Regulatory Authority (NVE-RME).* [Online]. Available from: https://publikasjoner.nve.no/rme_rapport/2021/rme_rapport2021_06.pdf 2023.03.01.

[20] Fornybar Norge. *24 strømleverandører sertifisert for Trygg strømhandel.* (24 energy providers certified for Safe electricity trading) [Online]. Available from: https://www.energinorge.no/nyheter/2021/24-stromleverandorer-sertifisert-for-trygg-stromhandel/ 2023.03.01.

[21] N. Albinson, S. Balaji, and Y. Chu, "Building digital trust: Technology can lead the way," Deloitte Insights, 2019. [Online]. Available from: https://www2.deloitte.com/content/dam/insights/us/articles/6320_Building-digital-trust/DI_Building-digital-trust.pdf 2023.03.01

[22] Olje- og energidepartementet. *Forskrift om måling, avregning, fakturering av nett tjenester og elektrisk energi, nettselskapets nøytralitet mv.* 1999 (Regulations on measurement, settlement, invoicing of network services and electrical energy, neutrality of the network company, etc. 1999) ([Online] Available from: https://lovdata.no/dokument/SF/forskrift/1999-03-11-301 2023.03.01

[23] M. Lotfi, C. Monteiro, M. Shafie-khah, and J. P. S. Catalão, "Transition toward blockchain-based electricity trading markets," in Blockchain-based Smart Grids, M. Shafie-khah, Ed. Academic Press, pp. 43-59, 2020.

[24] Q. Meng, L. Berntzen, B. Vesin, M. R. Johannessen, S. Opera, and A. Bara, "Blockchain Applications in Smart Grid – A Review and a Case Study" 18th European, Mediterranean, and Middle Eastern Conference on Information Systems (EMCIS), Lecture Notes in Business Information Processing 437, Springer, pp. 130-149, 2022.

[25] F. Ahmad and I. Huvila "Organizational changes, trust and information sharing: an empirical study", Aslib Journal of Information Management, Vol. 71(5), pp. 677-692. 2019.

[26] UK Department for Business, Innovation and Skills, *A Guide to Mutual Ownership Models.* November 2011. [Online]. Available from: https://assets.publishing.service.gov.uk/government/uploads/system/uploads/attachment_data/file/31678/11-1401-guide-mutual-ownership-models.pdf 2023.03.01.

[27] International Cooperative Alliance, *Cooperative identity, values & principles.* [Online]. Available from: https://www.ica.coop/en/cooperatives/cooperative-identity 2023.01.03

[28] K. D. Paine. *Guidelines for Measuring Trust in Organizations.* Institute for Public Relations [Online]. Available from: https://instituteforpr.org/guidelines-for-measuring-trust-in-organizations-2/, 2023.03.

[29] B. Lutz, "Plain Language: An Important Basis of E-Democracy and Open Government", Proceedings Conference for E-democracy and Open Government, (CEDEM) 2016, Danube University: Krems, Austria, 2016.

[30] S. K. Sonntag and L. Cardinal, "State traditions and Language Regimes: Conceptualizing Language Policy Choices," in State Traditions and Language regimes, S.K. Sonntag and L. Cardinal, Eds. McGill-Queen's University Press: Montreal & Kingston, pp. 3-28, 2015.

[31] M. Kvarenes, T. Reksten, I. Stranger-Thorsen, and L Aarønæs, "Klar, men aldri ferdig. En praktisk veileder i klarspråksarbeid, (Ready, but never finished. A practical guide in plain language work)," Språkrådet, 2011.

[32] M. Shardlow, "A survey of automated text simplification," International Journal of Advanced Computer Science and Applications, Special Issue on Natural Language Processing, pp. 58-70, 2014.

[33] M. R. Johannessen, L. Berntzen, and A. Ødegård, "A review of the Norwegian plain language policy," Proceedings 16th IFIP WG 8.5 International Conference on Electronic Government (EGOV), pp. 187-198, Springer, Cham., 2017.

[34] H. Haapio and T. D. Barton, "Business-friendly contracting: how simplification and visualization can help bring it to practice, "Liquid Legal, pp. 371-396, Springer, Cham., 2017.